Congressional Procedure

sunwΛter
INSTITUTE

Congressional Procedure

A Practical Guide to the Legislative Process in the U.S. Congress

Second Edition

RICHARD A. ARENBERG

Revised and Edited by Jeff Bozman

Hardback ISBN: 979-8-9926897-6-1

Paperback ISBN: 979-8-9926897-7-8

Ebook ISBN: 979-8-9926897-5-4

Cover and interior design: Andy Meaden, meadencreative.com

sunwʌter
I N S T I T U T E

The Sunwater Institute is a nonpartisan, nonprofit think tank based in North Bethesda, Maryland. Its mission is to strengthen the foundations of liberal democracy through interdisciplinary science, technology, and open dialogue.

The Sunwater Institute believes Congress's performance as an institution is critical to the wellbeing of the nation and democracy worldwide. It conducts theoretical and applied research aimed at improving Congress's institutional knowledge, processes, and efficiency.

The Sunwater Institute strives to convert lessons from its academic research projects into tools, analytics, datasets, publications, and trainings that are leveraged by governments, businesses, academia, media, and nonprofits.

Sunwater.org
Legis1.com

Contents

Dedications

From Richard Arenberg: For the love of my life, my wife of 20 years, Linda (Baron) Arenberg. Our first date was 54 years ago and she's even more beautiful and loving today.

From Jeff Bozman: In honor of Muftiah McCartin, and in memory of Paul Sarbanes, who both showed me Congress at its best.

About the Authors

Richard A. Arenberg is a Visiting Lecturer in Political Science and International and Public Affairs at Brown University. He previously taught at Northeastern University and Suffolk University. He worked for Sens. Paul Tsongas (D-MA), Carl Levin (D-MI), and Majority Leader George Mitchell (D-ME) for 34 years. He served on the Senate Iran-Contra Committee in 1987.

Arenberg is co-author of the award-winning *Defending the Filibuster: The Soul of the Senate*, named "Book of the Year in Political Science" by *Foreword Reviews* in 2012. A second edition was published in 2014. The U.S. Senate Historical Office published *Richard A. Arenberg: Oral History Interviews* in 2011.

He serves on the Board of Directors of Social Security Works and the Social Security Education Fund. He is an affiliate of the Taubman Center for American Politics and Policy. His work has appeared in *The New York Times, The Washington Post, The Providence Journal, Politico*, and *The Boston Globe*. He is also a contributor to *Newsmax* and *The Hill*. Arenberg holds bachelor's and master's degrees from Boston University.

Jeffrey T. Bozman has worked in all three branches of the federal government but counts his time on Capitol Hill as a professional highlight. He served as counsel to the chairman of the U.S. House Armed Services Committee from 2020 to 2022, where his portfolio encompassed Department of Defense acquisitions, industrial base policy, and foreign investment reviews.

From 2013 to 2020, Jeff practiced law with Covington & Burling in Washington, DC. At William & Mary Law School, Jeff served as Editor-in-Chief of the *Law Review* and was awarded the Thatcher Prize, the I'Anson Prize, and the Order of the Coif. He clerked for the Honorable Rebecca Beach Smith, then the Chief Judge of the U.S. District Court for the Eastern District of Virginia. Prior to law school, Jeff served as a Marine Corps officer.

Outside of legal practice, Jeff is a member of St. John's Church Lafayette Square and its choir. He was an early board member of the Armed Services Arts Partnership and a "plankowner" of the Lewis B. Puller, Jr., Veterans Benefits Clinic at William & Mary.

Acknowledgements

From Richard Arenberg: I worked in the Congress, mostly the Senate, for 34 years for three lions of the Senate of our era, George Mitchell, Carl Levin, and Paul Tsongas. I cannot find words adequate to express what I owe these three men. Each in their different way—and their style in the Senate was different—taught me numerous life lessons.

From Paul Tsongas, I learned it's OK to be absolutely candid, to say what's on your mind. In the end, truth could still turn out to be good politics and people will respect you for it.

From George Mitchell, I learned to take a step back from hard decisions to really weigh the arguments objectively and honestly. Hardest for me was learning to know when it's the right time to make a decision—when the issue has ripened.

And from Carl Levin, I learned it is possible to be the toughest bulldog around, demanding answers to important questions, accountability, and the highest ethical standards, while still being a warm, loving human being.

I came to Washington with Paul Tsongas filled with awe at the Congress; I never lost that sense of awe. On the very first day that we arrived in his new House office in 1975, then-Congressman Tsongas called me into his office. When the door was closed behind me, he impishly grinned, shrugged his shoulders, and asked, "Isn't this fun?" For the next 34 years, I never stopped asking myself Tsongas's question, and every day the answer was, "Yes, this is!"

Each day as I arrived, I looked up at the great dome of the Capitol and was inspired by that symbol. The first glimpse of that dome, especially lighted at night, as you proceed up Pennsylvania Avenue toward the West Front where every president from Reagan to Trump has taken the oath of office never fails to stir a sense of patriotism and the desire to be a part of what goes on there. In *Mr. Smith Goes to Washington*, Jimmy Stewart's character, a newly appointed senator, innocent, idealistic, and naïve, but infused with a sense of patriotism, catches his first glimpse of the Capitol dome and cries out, "Look! Look! There it is!"

In the words of Winston Churchill, "We shape our buildings; thereafter, they shape us." It was ultimately the people I met and worked with during my years on Capitol Hill that fuel my continuing faith in the resiliency of the Congress as the protector of our freedoms and the rule of law in the face of all evidence to the contrary.

I owe a debt of gratitude to Brown University, which has given me a better academic landing place than I could have hoped for. In my last years on the Senate staff, I thought often about what "life after the Senate" would be like for me.

"What," I thought, "does one do with decades of experience that is applicable in so few places?" Many of my colleagues "went downtown," meaning they became lobbyists. That wasn't for me. That is not why I came to Washington. I am a "true believer," and I came to get things done.

I began thinking, if only some university would allow me to share my experience and insight with a classroom full of bright, engaged students wanting to do something in the world of public policy and politics, it would suit me perfectly. I had no idea if anyone would.

Then Professor Marion Orr, then the Director of the Taubman Center at Brown University, called. It was Thanksgiving of 2008. He asked, "Can you be here to teach a course in January?" I was not really yet ready to retire from the Senate. After all, Barack Obama had just been elected, and the Democrats in the Senate were about to have a filibuster-proof majority, something I had never experienced. But, Brown is Brown. I knew its reputation and I thought, "This is the perfect place for me."

When I was first making the decision to leave Washington, my academic friends said, "You don't really want to do this. You are used to being a 'big shot' on Capitol Hill. In academia, as an 'adjunct,' no one will respect you."

Nothing could have turned out to be further from the truth. I have benefited from the encouragement and wise advice of many colleagues at Brown. Never have I felt disrespected; to the contrary, I have seen that the practical experience I brought with me is valued by my colleagues and students.

I want to thank Marion Orr, who I have already mentioned, and Jim Morone, who first brought me into the Political Science Department, and the many Brown colleagues who have encouraged and supported me. However, I owe particular thanks to my friend, Political Science Department Chair Wendy Schiller, for her unfailing encouragement in my fledgling attempts to be an academic.

For the past nine years, I have taught at Brown University in both the Political Science Department and the Watson Institute for International and Public Affairs, about the Congress, the presidency, campaigns and elections, political communication, and the political process. Here, too, I have found hope in the future of our democracy. I have interacted with many hundreds of bright and capable students interested and engaged in public policy. It is often their enthusiasm for learning that drives me forward. A number are already working in positions on Capitol Hill or have sought elective office on their own. I am proud of this little "Arenberg caucus."

Being at Brown has given me the freedom to speak in my own voice. As a Senate staffer, one must always weigh the impact that one's own words might have on the senator for whom you work. Whatever you do, it is seen as a reflection on the senator. I miss the rough and tumble of Capitol Hill every single day, but I never regret the decision to come to Brown.

This book, like my first, *Defending the Filibuster: The Soul of the Senate* that I wrote with former Senate parliamentarian Bob Dove, is a product of that freedom.

I am indebted to my support group of former "hill rats" who together cumulatively account for more than two centuries of congressional experience. They shared their special expertise to straighten me out when my writing veered off course or got it wrong.

This book could not have been written without the sage advice of the Senate Parliamentarian Emeritus, Alan Frumin. Alan and I served together in the Senate in very different capacities for more than three decades. His office as parliamentarian was always open to me for my eager questions about procedure and the rules of the Senate. As my long-time dear friend, he has graciously given of his time and expertise to scrub my books, many of my op-eds, and for the past five years has come to Providence to deliver guest lectures in my classes at Brown. On a number of occasions, we have shared the stage or appeared together on television programs and at lectures. I am deeply grateful for his friendship and his willingness to improve my work writing about the Congress. No one knows the rules and precedents of the Senate better than Alan Frumin.

Donald Ritchie, Historian Emeritus of the United States Senate, also read and commented on each chapter as it was written. He has been unfailingly supportive and helps to strengthen my confidence that I have a credible historical perspective on the Senate. Don is a gifted oral historian and spent three days some years ago interviewing me for the Senate Historical Office's Oral History collection, an experience I treasure.

Always, it is Kaye Meier on whom I rely for the first reading of each chapter. She is a valued friend and former colleague whose smart edits and reliably upbeat assessments propelled this book forward. Kaye served as Legislative Director to Senator Barbara Boxer (D-CA) and Senior Counsel to Senator Carl Levin (D-MI).

Alex Harman served as the Obama Administration White House Liaison for the Department of Homeland Security, Chief Counsel to Sen. Mazie Hirono (D-HI), Chief of Staff to Congressman Steven Horsford (D-NV-4), and General Counsel to Sen. Mark Udall (D-CO) (he also worked for Sens. Bayh [D-IN], Kennedy [D-MA], and Reid [D-NV]). Alex, a friend and kindred spirit, gave freely of his time and I am indebted to him for his perceptive comments.

Joe Bryan served as Deputy Assistant Secretary of the Navy and as Professional Staff for the Senate Armed Services Committee, the Senate Select Committee on Intelligence, the Senate Permanent Subcommittee on Investigations, and as a legislative assistant to both Sen. Carl Levin (D-MI) and Congressman John Lewis (D-GA). I hired Joe for Senator Levin's staff and could not have made a better choice. A friend for many years now, Joe brought a wealth of experience and perspective to his edits and advice.

My friends Elise Bean and Linda Gustitus were both enormously helpful and made numerous suggestions that strengthened the sections on congressional oversight and investigations, a subject on which Elise and Linda are nationally known experts. Both Elise and Linda served as Staff Director of the Senate Permanent Subcommittee on Investigations (Linda also was previously Staff Director of two other subcommittees). Currently, Elise and Linda are Co-Directors of the Levin Center at Wayne Law, focused on improving public policy by strengthening in-depth, bipartisan oversight of public and private sector activities by the Congress and other legislative bodies. It was Linda Gustitus who first suggested I write this book.

Mark Cruz, a former graduate student of mine at Brown University, who is Chief of Staff to Congressman Todd Rokita (R-IN), made a number of useful suggestions regarding descriptions of procedures on the floor of the House of Representatives.

This is a better book for the generous efforts of all of these people.

However, this book would never have been written but for the fact that Chug Roberts of TheCapitol.Net reached out to me and encouraged me to write it. Chug and Karen Hormuth, Executive Director of TheCapitol.Net, have been a pleasure to work with and very patient when my estimates of how long the manuscript might take proved too ambitious.

I am proud to be published by TheCapitol.Net, which has produced a long list of excellent publications about Congress. TheCapitol.Net also does an unparalleled job helping to educate congressional staff, federal employees, state and local officials, foreign delegations, college students, and many others who work with or around the Congress and need to be better informed about how it operates.

I love the Congress. Much of my adult life was dedicated to working with senators whom I admired greatly. I hope this book will impart some of that admiration and affection—and concern—to the reader.

Finally, I am especially grateful for the love and support that I receive from my family, especially my children, Josh, Georgina, Meg and Ned and grandsons, Ethan, Owen, and Noah. And most important is the endless strength I derive, and enthusiasm I receive from my wife of twenty years, but soulmate of more than fifty years, Linda, to whom I have dedicated this book.

From Jeff Bozman: I thank Matt Chervenak and the Sunwater team for the opportunity to revise this book. My only disagreement with Professor Arenberg's lovely introduction is the suggestion that lobbyists don't "get things done." My path to professional staff service on the Hill had a few detours after my days as an undergraduate intern for Senator Sarbanes, including a seven-year stint downtown. When I returned to DC in 2013 as a newly minted lawyer, I had the privilege of working with Covington's public policy group. Muftiah McCartin, Roger Zakheim, Samantha Clark, Joan Kutcher, Jack Schenendorf, John Veroneau, and many others with esteemed public service backgrounds showed me how much good a private practitioner can do. More importantly, they took me under their care and gave me the support and confidence to learn the craft of legislative advocacy. I write this book with a slightly heavier ratio of private sector to public sector work, in the hopes that it is useful for new practitioners of all types, whether in or out of government.

I am indebted to Professor Arenberg's scholarly first edition. I have streamlined, updated, and adjusted the text to reflect developments in policy, law, and politics since it was published. I have also removed some internal cross references and links, and instead encourage practitioners to take advantage of the expanded public access to outstanding Congressional Research Service analysis for deeper examination of many topics addressed here.

Revising this book during a turbulent time in electoral politics has been a balm, and a reminder of the profound good that elected officeholders, staff members, and advocates can do through legislation. I have enjoyed the close study of this craft and hope readers find useful and helpful perspectives in these pages.

Preface

The Founders had high hopes for Congress. They created the institution in Article I of the new Constitution in 1789. The first section of that first article establishes the Congress and confers sweeping legislative powers: "All legislative Powers herein granted shall be vested in a Congress of the United States, which shall consist of a Senate and House of Representatives." The powers of Congress are so extensively laid out that Article I takes up more space in the Constitution than Articles II through VII combined.

The Founders set up the elaborate system of checks and balances to assure that no one branch of government could dominate, but most of the Framers fully expected the legislative branch to play the lead role. James Madison in *The Federalist* No. 51 wrote, "In republican government, the legislative authority necessarily predominates."

Yet, throughout our history, the American people have been skeptical of Congress and the legislative body has suffered in the eyes of the American people. In 1897, Mark Twain wrote, "It could probably be shown by facts and figures that there is no native criminal class except Congress." Former Congressman Mo Udall (D-AZ) loved to tell the tale of a constituent who wrote to him, "Of all the rats and snakes elected to represent the people and carry out their wishes, you rank head and shoulders beneath the lowest."

Congressional approval ratings have been reliably low since the beginning of public opinion polling in the United States in the 1940s, dipping as low as 9% approval in November 2013. With the exception of the nation's reaction in the wake of the September 11 attacks when the approval of Congress doubled virtually overnight to 84%, Americans have held the institution of Congress in low regard. The Gallup Poll historical average is about 33%.

Former Senate Majority Leader George Mitchell (D-ME) said, "The attitude of the public toward elected officials in American democracy has always been one of skepticism…"

Legislative bodies in democracies typically suffer the same fate. Sir A. J. Herbert, a member of the British Parliament and a humorist, wrote a wonderful book titled *The Point of Parliament* in 1946 as a child's guide to Parliament. Although he was discussing the British Parliament and not the American Congress and there is lightheartedness to his descriptions, Herbert sheds light on the unpopularity of legislative bodies:

> …I remind you that we have been fighting for freedom, which includes free speech and free parliaments. So you would expect to hear from time to time, a kindly reference to our own free Parliament and its members. But no. …[M]embers of Parliament are known as "politicians" and politicians, with the possible exception of journalists, are the lowest form of serpent life.

Sound familiar?

George Mitchell cautioned:

> It is a mistake to think of politics as something separate and apart from the rest of society. Politics are subject to the same influences. …These influences of modern life—technology communications and changing standards in public life and the media—have led to a decline in public trust and confidence that is felt by all of our major institutions. …Congress has been a particular recipient of current negative attitudes because it is so prominent, public, and focused on by the media.

The mainstream media is attracted to the drama and personalities of the partisan warfare on Capitol Hill. Much less coverage is focused on the understanding of the nitty-gritty of how Congress actually works.

For most American citizens and immigrants, Congress is a black box. They can see much of what goes in, and what comes out, but the process in the box is opaque.

This book will attempt to open that black box and examine the machinery in a way that is accurate but accessible. It seeks to educate the layman and average voters, but also hopefully to contribute to a fuller understanding of congressional procedure by students in the classroom and those who deal directly with the legislative branch, and perhaps even some within it.

Woodrow Wilson called lawmaking "the dance of legislation." He added, "It is not surprising…that the enacting, revising, tinkering, repealing of laws should engross the attention and engage the entire energy of such a body as the Congress."

Even members themselves who too often yield leverage and power that they might otherwise wield, simply because they do not know the rules, may benefit. Former Congressman John Dingell (D-MI), who served in Congress longer than any member, 59 years, said, "I'll let you write the substance… you let me write the procedure, and I'll screw you every time."

Procedures matter. The protector of stability, comity, and fair play in the House and the Senate is procedure.

We are familiar with the many ways in which Congress has been dysfunctional, but in fundamental ways the Congress has proved both stable and resilient. We should remember that the central hopes around which the Constitution was built include the protection of liberty and the rule of law.

Senator George Mitchell, speaking in 1998, pointed out that:

> …the men who wrote the American Constitution had as their overriding objective the prevention of tyranny in America. They had lived under a British king; they did not want ever to have to live under an American king. They placed the highest value on individual liberty. In retrospect we can see they were brilliantly successful. We have had forty-two presidents and no kings. Americans enjoy a combination of personal freedom and shared material prosperity that is without parallel in the world, and arguably without parallel in

human history. Therefore, who is to say that the institutions created by the Constitution don't work?

Nearly 250 years into the experiment, Congress continues to succeed at that.

A glossary of terms relating to Congress, its procedures, and related institutions follows the concluding chapter.

Chapter 1
Congress and the Constitution

Table of Sections

A. Introduction

The Constitutional Convention called together in Philadelphia in 1787 was merely expected to amend the Articles of Confederation to repair its defects arising principally from the weakness of the central government that it created. Among the Articles' inadequate provisions was the Congress they created, a weak and incompetent body beholden to the states for many of the essential functions of national government. The Convention undertook to create a new Constitution.

The Founders created a new Congress in the first Article of the Constitution. The bicameral institution they designed includes the House of Representatives and the Senate. Article I, Section 1 declares: "All legislative Powers herein granted shall be vested in a Congress of the United States, which shall consist of a Senate and House of Representatives."

The Founders had high hopes for Congress. They understood that a strong legislature is fundamental to a healthy democracy. At the same time, they feared a central government that was too powerful. To restrain that power they created a Constitution that divides power among the branches of the federal government (separation of powers) and between the federal government and the states (federalism).

They set up a system of checks and balances among the three branches of the federal government (executive, legislative, and judicial) to assure that no one co-equal branch could dominate. At the founding, however, the Constitution gave Congress the most institutional power of any branch.

Of course, the way Congress is organized and its procedures play a huge part in public policy decisions and outcomes. The division of Congress into two chambers with differing structures was intended to create bodies with different roles. James Madison explained in *The Federalist* No. 51 that the legislature was itself divided "into different branches; and to render them, by different modes of election and different principles of action, as little connected with each other as the nature of their common functions and their common dependence on the society will admit."

The design purposely created one chamber, the House, to be closer and more immediately responsive to the electorate, and another chamber, the Senate, to be more insulated from the winds of popular opinion. In the famous, probably apocryphal story often used to illuminate this difference, George Washington explained the need for a Senate to Thomas Jefferson. Jefferson, who was in France during the deliberations of the Constitutional Convention, asked why a second body, an "upper body," was even necessary. Washington is said to have compared the Senate to a saucer, used to sip from in order to cool the hot tea poured from the cup in the polite society of the day.

The House of Representatives, the dispenser of "hot tea," is sometimes referred to as "the People's House." Given shorter terms of office (2 years) and smaller and usually more homogenous constituencies than the Senate (6 years), the House was expected to act more quickly in response to public opinion. The House has developed rules that provide the ability for a majority to respond in this way. The House is a majoritarian institution. Even a single-vote majority gives vastly more power to the party in the majority than the party in the minority.

The Senate, Washington's "cooling saucer," by contrast is sometimes referred to as the "world's greatest deliberative body." James Madison referred to the Senate as a "necessary fence" against the "fickleness and passion" of the popular will and the members of the House of Representatives. The Senate remains a chamber where negotiation and compromise reign; without a supermajority, no one party can dominate the Senate the way it can the House.

Like other checks and balances in the Constitution, the division of Congress into two separate and different chambers serves to protect against the concentration of power within Congress. The Framers nonetheless expected that the legislative branch would prove to be the most powerful of the three branches. As Madison argued in the Federalist Papers, the legislative branch "necessarily predominates." To guard against the concentration of legislative power, the Founders created a system in which neither chamber is able to make laws alone.

B. Constitutional Provisions

The Constitution, in Article I, extensively lays out the powers of Congress. Central to the congressional role is the grant of "all legislative powers" and the "power of the purse." At the Constitutional Convention in 1787, Massachusetts delegate Elbridge Gerry (later James Madison's vice president) argued that the House of Representatives "was more immediately the representatives of the people, and it was a maxim that the people ought to hold the purse-strings."

Article I, Section 8 lists a number of specific powers. Among the enumerated powers are the power to lay and collect taxes and pay the debts (Clause 1), borrow money on credit (Clause 2), regulate commerce with foreign nations and among the states (Clause 3), create the courts below the Supreme Court (which is created in Article III) (Clause 9), raise and support an army (Clause 12) and navy (Clause 13), declare war (Clause 11), and others.

Clause 18, the Necessary and Proper Clause, gives the power "[t]o make all laws which shall be necessary and proper for carrying into Execution the [other listed] Powers." This authority is sometimes referred to as the "Elastic Clause" because it gives flexibility to Congress in exercising the powers that are separately enumerated.

Article I takes up more space in the Constitution than Articles II through VII combined. By comparison, the descriptions of presidential powers (Article II) and those of the courts (Article III) are less precisely stated. They are, however, expansively and categorically stated: "The executive Power" is vested solely in the President. "The judicial Power" is vested in the Supreme Court, and subordinate federal courts that the Framers allowed Congress to establish. The precise scope and contours of those powers remain debated well into the twenty-first century.

Among the provisions of the Constitution affecting the Congress, several are of particular importance.

Article I, Section 2 stipulates two-year terms and sets the necessary qualifications for members of the House. Section 3 does the same for senators, creating six-year terms and the qualifications for senators.

Article I, Section 7, Clause 1, commonly referred to as the "Origination Clause," states, "All Bills for raising Revenue shall originate in the House of Representatives; but the Senate may propose or concur with Amendments as on other Bills." The Framers gave the "power of the purse," as James Madison referred to it, to Congress, specifically to the House of Representatives.

Madison wrote in *The Federalist Papers*, No. 58, "The House of Representatives cannot only refuse, but they alone can propose, the supplies requisite for the support of the government. ... This power over the purse may, in fact, be regarded as the most complete and effectual weapon with which any constitution can arm the immediate representatives of the people."

The House enforces this constitutional prerogative through the use of a process called the "blue slip." In the event that the Senate passes a revenue bill and sends it to the House, any member of the House may offer a resolution that the Senate bill violates the prerogatives of the House under the Origination Clause of the Constitution. Such resolutions are routinely adopted, often by voice vote, and the bill is returned to the Senate.

The blue slip takes its name from the fact that the message returning the bill to Senate is blue. This is, however, a bit of a misnomer since all messages from the House to the Senate are on blue paper.

The House has historically viewed "revenue bill" broadly to include tax and other revenue bills, as well as appropriations measures that spend government funds. The Senate interprets "revenue bill" more narrowly and contests the inclusion of appropriations bills. However, the blue slip process has rendered Senate objections on this point relatively toothless. Blue slip issues can arise in legislation that purports to levy monetary penalties or sanctions. In 2018, the House raised concerns late in the conference process of the Fiscal Year 2019 National Defense Authorization Act over restrictions on its authority to modify penalties on a Chinese technology company.

Central to the independence of Congress are the protections provided by Article I, Section 6. Senators and representatives are not subject to arrest during sessions or when travelling to those sessions (with the exception of arrests for treason, felonies, or the breach of the peace). Further, the "Speech and Debate Clause" prohibits questioning of members of Congress in any other place regarding what they say on the floor of the House or Senate.

Article I, Section 6 also stipulates that no member, while serving in Congress, may hold any other federal office. As a result, when senators or representatives are appointed to the cabinet, for example, they must resign their congressional office before taking the oath for their new position.

One additional noteworthy congressional power is granted in Article II. In Section 4, the Constitution provides that the president (vice president and other civil officers) may be removed from office "on impeachment for, and conviction of, treason, bribery, or other high crimes and misdemeanors." Earlier, in Article I, Section 2, the Constitution states that it is the House of Representatives that has the "sole power of impeachment." Section 3 then grants the sole power to "try all impeachments" to the Senate. The Chief Justice of the United States presides over an impeachment trial of a president in the Senate, and a two-thirds vote of senators present is required for conviction and removal. The House has voted to impeach a president four times: Andrew Jackson in 1868; Bill Clinton in 1998; and Donald Trump in both 2019 and 2021. In each case, the president was acquitted by the Senate (in the final case, after he had left the office of the presidency). In 1974, Richard Nixon resigned the presidency in the face of what appeared to be certain impeachment by the House and subsequent conviction by the Senate.

The Constitution has been amended to provide additional power to the Congress. In 1967, the Twenty-Fifth Amendment was ratified. In the event of a vacancy in the office of the vice president, it provides for the nomination by the president and confirmation by a majority vote in each chamber of Congress of an individual to fill that vacancy. The Amendment also creates a procedure for the vice president to become acting president if the vice president and a majority of the cabinet declare the president unable to discharge his powers and duties. It further prescribes a process for resolving the matter if a president asserts, contrary to such a declaration, that they are capable of discharging their duties. Under these circumstances, the president would resume their powers and duties unless by a two-thirds vote of each chamber, Congress determines the president is unable to do so.

Under Article V of the Constitution, Congress plays a central role in adopting amendments to the Constitution by a two-thirds vote of each chamber ratified by three-fourths of the state legislatures.

C. Rules

Perhaps one of the most critical protections of congressional independence and power is Article I, Section 5 of the Constitution, which states in part, "Each House may determine the Rules of its Proceedings...." Pursuant to this provision the House and the Senate have developed very different rules. Those rules have established the character of each chamber in ways that enhance their constitutional design.

The House of Representatives adopts its rules at the outset of every new term of Congress (every two years). These changes can be minimal from the previous Congress. When control of the House changes parties, the rules changes are more likely to be extensive. For example, in 1995, when House Republicans became the majority for the first time in forty years, newly elected Speaker Newt Gingrich (R-GA) led the Republican Conference to a major overhaul of the House rules.

The rules of the House are adopted by majority vote. The rules, precedents, procedure, customs, and mores of the House serve to protect the principle of majority rule.

The formal rules are set down in the *House Rules and Manual*, which contains the foundation for the parliamentary procedure followed by the House, including the adopted rules of the House, portions of Jefferson's Manual, the Constitution, relevant adopted resolutions, and House precedents, which are rulings made by the Speaker and other presiding officers.

The House Committee on Rules is an extremely powerful standing committee of the House, previously known as the "Speaker's Committee" for its function as an arm of House leadership, and the instrument by which the Speaker controls the House floor. The Rules Committee typically has a supermajority of members from the majority party. In 2025, the Rules Committee summarized its power on its website: "The Committee has the authority to do virtually anything during the course of consideration of a measure, including deeming it passed.... In essence, so long as a majority of the House is willing to vote for a special rule, there is little that the Rules Committee cannot do."

The Senate Standing Rules, precedents, and practices are designed to protect legislative minorities and the rights of individual senators. The parliamentary procedure of a "previous question motion" typically allows a body to cut off debate and move to a substantive vote. The rules adopted by the first Senate provided for a previous question motion, effectively allowing a senator to limit debate by moving the previous question by simple majority vote. That provision was dropped in 1806, and the filibuster—a powerful tool for the minority—became a defining characteristic of Senate debate. The House of Representatives has a "previous question" rule: when a member moves the previous question by saying "I move the previous question," and the motion is agreed to, debate and further amendment is ended and the House moves to a vote on the matter before it. Most legislative bodies have such a motion in their rules.

Today we understand such motions as requiring an end to debate and an immediate vote on the pending matter. In the House of Representatives this motion to cut off debate requires only a simple majority vote.

The absence of such a rule in the Senate now permits what is commonly known as the filibuster. Filibusters, which are characterized by extended debate and/or other dilatory tactics, can be ended under Senate Rule XXII through a process called "cloture," requiring a supermajority of three fifths of the senators duly chosen and sworn, 60 votes (with some exceptions). This has a broad range of implications because it requires the majority in many circumstances to consult or negotiate with the minority even in the routine workings of the Senate. Proposals to relax, reform, or even eliminate the filibuster have prompted fierce debates among senators and observers of the institution. In the past fifteen years, the filibuster has essentially disappeared as a tool for the minority party to block presidential nominations that require "advice and consent" of the Senate.

While the early Senate rules included a previous question motion, the evidence is that it served a different purpose. A scholarly essay by Johns Hopkins University Professor Joseph Cooper concludes that the previous question as it existed in the early Senate of 1789–1806 "was not designed to operate as a cloture mechanism…it was not in practice used as a cloture mechanism" and "it is even improbable that the Senate could have used the previous question for cloture."

Unlike the House, where the rules can and frequently do change with each Congress, the Senate adopted its rules in 1789 and although they have been amended and codified, the basic rules have been continuously in place. Because the Senate considers itself a "continuing body" it does not adopt its rules at the beginning of each Congress. This is based on the fact that only one-third of senators stand for election for each term of Congress (one-third of the senators are to be elected every two years, "divided as equally as may be into three Classes" [Article I, Section 3, Clause 2]). Since the remaining two-thirds are already "chosen and sworn" and since a quorum in the Senate, under the Constitution, is a majority, there is no period of time during which a quorum of the Senate does not exist.

Even though Senate rules can be changed by a simple majority vote, the Senate rules that continue from one Congress to another do require a two-thirds majority of senators voting to end debate on any rules change.

D. Congressional Terms, Recesses, and Sessions

Each term of Congress lasts for a two year period from January 3rd of odd-numbered years. Terms are commonly divided into two "sessions" of Congress, although more are possible, either convened by the Congress or by the president calling Congress back into session. The president—under Article II, Section 3—is granted the power to "on extraordinary Occasions, convene both Houses, or either of them, and in Case of Disagreement between them, with Respect to the Time of Adjournment, he may adjourn them to such Time as he shall think proper." The scope of the president's power to do so has not been fully tested in litigation. Before the start of the second Trump administration, commentators explored the clause in relation to its impact on a president's ability to make "recess appointments" of individuals whose positions are subject to Senate confirmation. In extreme cases, the clause could theoretically allow a president to appoint controversial nominees who would serve for nearly two years, without the advice and consent of the Senate. The Supreme Court has, however, held "that, for purposes of the Recess Appointments Clause, the Senate is in session when it says it is, provided that, under its own rules, it retains the capacity to transact Senate business." The Court further concluded that "a recess of more than 3 days but less than 10 days is presumptively too short to fall within the [Recess Appointments] Clause." In any event, a congressional session ends when the Congress adjourns "*sine die*," Latin meaning "without any day" set to reconvene.

When a Congress plans to reconvene a second session following the general election in November of even numbered years, it does not adjourn *sine die*. The period after the election up to the *sine die* adjournment at the end of that second session is popularly referred to as a "lame-duck session."

The transition from the first session to the second session, at the end of the first calendar year of a given Congress, ends the consideration of nominations, but has no effect on the progress of legislative matters.

However, when the Congress adjourns *sine die* at the end of the two-year term, all legislative matters die. Therefore, in order to advance any bill or resolution in the next Congress, it must be reintroduced. An exception is treaties submitted to the Senate by the president for ratification, which carry over from one Congress to the next.

E. Members of Congress

The Constitution stipulates in Article I, Section 2, that the House of Representatives must have at least one representative from each state. Further, it provides that members of the House serve two-year terms, must be at least 25 years old, have been a U.S. citizen for at least seven years, and must reside in the state (although not necessarily the district) from which they are elected.

Article I, Section 3 states that each state is represented in the Senate by two senators, elected for six-year terms, who must be at least 30 years old, have been a citizen for at least nine years, and must also be a resident of the state from which they are elected.

Congressional elections occur every two years. Since members of the House serve two-year terms, all of the House of Representatives is elected in each congressional election.

By contrast, senators serve six-year terms. The Constitution established a rotation in which one of three "classes" of senators is elected at each congressional election. This means that only one-third of the Senate stands for election every two years. Article I, Section 3 of the Constitution stipulated that senators would be "chosen" by individual state legislatures. The Seventeenth Amendment, ratified in 1913, changed the process and provided for direct election of senators in each state "by the people thereof."

The House currently consists of 435 members, a total set by law in 1913 and reaffirmed by the Permanent Apportionment Act of 1929. The District of Columbia is represented by a non-voting delegate. In addition, Guam, the

Virgin Islands, American Samoa, and the Northern Mariana Islands each have one delegate. Puerto Rico is represented by a resident commissioner. These six representatives do not vote on final passage of matters on the House floor, but possess all other powers of members.

Members of the House represent districts drawn by their states, which are roughly proportional to population based on the census that the Constitution requires to be conducted every ten years. In some states, district lines have been drawn to benefit the political party that controls the state legislature, a practice known as "gerrymandering."

California, the nation's largest state, as measured in the 2020 census, is represented by 52 members of Congress, while Alaska, Delaware, Montana, North Dakota, South Dakota, Vermont, and Wyoming have only one representative, representing the entire state "at large."

There are 100 senators, two from each state. This equality of state representation in the Senate was the product of the "Great Compromise" at the Constitutional Convention in 1787. Small states pressed for equal representation in Congress and the larger states sought proportional representation for both chambers of Congress. The compromise created one chamber based on each principle. As a result, Wyoming (the least populous state as of 2024) has the same representation in the Senate as California, with less than 2 percent of California's population.

That compromise was deemed so fundamental to the establishment of a federal government that it cannot be changed using the normal means of amending the Constitution. Article V states, "no state, without its consent, shall be deprived of its equal suffrage in the Senate."

Members of the House and Senate may only be removed from office by a two-thirds vote of members voting, a quorum having been established, of the Senate (if a senator) or the House (if a representative). (The Constitution defines a quorum in Article I, Section 5: "...a Majority of each [chamber] shall constitute a Quorum to do Business.") There is no recall provision allowing for removal of members of Congress by popular vote prior to regularly scheduled congressional elections.

F. House of Representatives

The House of Representatives is a majoritarian body. This means that the House is ruled strictly, at most times, by majority vote.

Under the Constitution, Article I, Section 4 (as amended by the Twentieth Amendment), "The Congress shall assemble at least once in every Year." Under that provision the first meeting of each Congress "shall begin at noon on the 3d day of January, unless they shall by law appoint a different day."

Vacancies in the House are filled by special elections (Article I, Section 2). There is no provision for appointment of members to the House.

Regarding leadership, Article I, Section 2 of the Constitution states, "The House of Representatives shall chuse their Speaker..." This is done by majority vote of the whole body at the outset of each new Congress. Party caucuses nominate candidates, and the election normally takes place between the nominees of the Democratic and Republican caucuses, respectively. On occasion the names of additional candidates are placed in nomination.

Under existing law, the Speaker is second in the line of succession to the presidency, behind the vice-president, in the event of the president's death or disability.

House party leaders, the majority leader, the minority leader, the majority whip, the minority whip, and others are elected by majority vote of the respective party caucuses. At the beginning of each Congress, the leadership is elected on the first day.

The Speaker is the presiding officer of the House. Speakers have, in the past, viewed themselves as leaders of the whole House, as well as party leaders, and have protected that distinction. Rep. Bob Michel (R-IL), who served as minority leader for 14 years—from 1981 to 1995—but never became the Speaker, described the role of Speaker as, "...by history, tradition and rule the leader of the whole House, not the majority, not the minority, but the whole. The Speaker must drop the mantle of partisanship the day he assumes office."

As the House has become more partisan, Speakers have been increasingly viewed primarily as party leaders. Michel contrasted his comfortable relationship with Democratic Speakers Tip O'Neill (D-MA) and Tom Foley (D-WA) with the much more vitriolic relationships of minority leaders with later Speakers like Newt Gingrich (R-GA), Nancy Pelosi (D-CA), John Boehner (R-OH), and Paul Ryan (R-WI). Michel observed in 2008, "With Tom and Tip, ye gads, we got along. Sure, we had our doggone partisan differences; I expect that. You can't be namby-pamby about it. But when push came to shove, or during a real nitty-gritty situation, why, I always knew that I could talk with either one of them on a simply man-to-man basis and no holds barred. And that's a good feeling to have."

By tradition, the Speaker normally does not cast a vote. When the Speaker votes, it underlines the importance of the measure in question.

The Speaker, as the presiding officer, under House rules has the power (sometimes delegated to other senior members of the majority) to recognize members to speak or make motions on the floor. The Speaker, acting with the advice of House officers and party leaders, refers legislation to committees of jurisdiction and names members of conference committees with the Senate. Conference committees are temporary joint committees appointed to resolve differences between the chambers on a measure passed by each.

The Speaker is also afforded powers by the majority caucus, including a central role in the assignment of members to committees, particularly to the powerful Rules Committee. The Speaker, as a practical matter, controls what legislation is scheduled on the House floor.

The powers given to the Speaker are intended to assure that if they can marshal the votes of the majority caucus, the Speaker is able to largely control the legislative outcomes in the House. When sizeable factions oppose a Speaker in their own party, such control is in doubt. The Speaker's job is particularly challenging when the majority party's margin in the House is narrow, or when the majority is ideologically divided.

Neither the Speaker nor the president *pro tempore* of the Senate is constitutionally required to be a member of Congress, although historically all have been.

The House majority leader is second in the line of party leadership. They work with the Speaker on the legislative agenda and play a key role in persuading members of the caucus to follow the leadership.

The House minority leader heads the minority party and is the chief strategist in articulating the views of the minority party, frequently in opposition to the majority. They lead the minority's efforts to influence legislation. If the Speaker is able to keep the majority party in line, it can be difficult in the majoritarian House for the minority to have much effective input. However, the Speaker often must rely upon members of the minority to pass legislation, especially when a majority is narrow and factions within the majority party are willing to vote against the Speaker. Recent examples have arisen frequently in the past decade in connection with legislation to raise the debt ceiling and avoid a default of debts owed by the federal government.

Both parties elect a whip, third in the line of majority leadership and second among the minority leadership. The party whips, alongside their staff and deputies, lead vote-counting organizations on their respective sides of the aisle. The main role of the whips and their offices is to provide a channel of communication between the leadership and rank and file members. This is important to keep leaders informed of the various views in the caucus, to assist in persuading rank and file members to support the party position, and to keep track of the likely vote count.

Others members of the House leadership include the chairs of the Democratic Caucus and the Republican Conference. These two organizations serve as primary vehicles for communicating their respective party's message on policy and legislation. Also in the leadership are the chairs of the National Republican Congressional Committee (NRCC) and Democratic Congressional Campaign Committee (DCCC), the political campaign arms of the Congressional Republican and Democratic caucuses.

They recruit candidates for House races across the country and raise and distribute campaign money to them.

G. Senate

Senators serve longer terms and represent larger, more diverse state-wide constituencies. Two key procedural characteristics in the Senate distinguish its legislative practice: unlimited debate and nearly unfettered amendment.

The Senate rules and precedents governing debate and the offering of amendments are fundamental to the protection of legislative minorities.

The right to debate, enforced primarily by the existence of the filibuster, means that much of the routine activity of the Senate requires unanimous consent (because the alternative is so time-consuming and burdensome). Much of the business in the Senate, both routine and consequential, is conducted through "unanimous consent agreements," often negotiated between the party leaders or their designees. The ability of a single senator to slow down or even prevent the Senate from doing business can make the Senate a very difficult body to lead.

Increasingly the political polarization of the Senate and efforts by the minority to use procedure to obstruct the majority or by the majority to circumvent the minority have rendered these procedural rules more controversial.

James Madison wrote in *Notes of Debates in the Federal Convention of 1787* (June 26, 1787):

> In order to judge of the form to be given to [the Senate], it will be proper to take a view of the ends to be served by it. These were first to protect the people against their rulers: secondly to protect the people against the transient impressions into which they themselves might be led.

Senate vacancies are filled differently depending on the respective state's election laws. In contrast to how House vacancies may be filled, most states permit temporary appointment of senators, usually until the next scheduled congressional election. Some states, however, require a special election (with or without provision for a temporary appointment until that special election).

Article I, Section 3 designates the vice president of the United States as president of the Senate, and stipulates that the vice president is to have no vote in the Senate except in the case of a tie. Section 3 also authorizes the selection of a president *pro tempore* to serve in the absence of the vice president.

The president *pro tempore* or their designee presides over the Senate when the vice president is not present. From the first Senate, senators have retained the important powers and kept the presiding officer of the body weak—the vice president comes from the executive branch and may not be of the same party as the Senate majority. Rulings by the presiding officer may be overturned in the Senate by majority vote. As a result, the president *pro tempore*'s role is likewise relatively weak and largely honorific. The tradition in the Senate has been to elect the most senior member of the majority party to the position. This means that this officer, under current law behind only the vice president and the Speaker of the House in the presidential line of succession, can be more than eighty or ninety years old.

The Senate majority leader, elected among his or her peers in the majority, is generally regarded as the "first among equals." The position carries few constitutional powers. By precedent and in practice, however, the majority leader is given the "right of first recognition." This means that although the Senate rules require the presiding officer to recognize the senator who first seeks recognition, when the majority leader is among those seeking it, that leader will be recognized. This, along with the power to decide the Senate's agenda (even that requires negotiation with the minority leader because of the Senate rules of debate) are the principle tools the majority leader uses to "control" the Senate.

Notwithstanding the powers of the majority leader, little can be accomplished, even in the routine operation of the Senate, without negotiating with the minority leader. Former Majority Leader George Mitchell (D-ME) described this fact as creating "a near-permanent state of negotiation. With its checks and balances the Senate is a microcosm of the American system itself … It's relatively easy to obstruct and prevent things from occurring. It's very difficult to gain enactment."

As a practical matter, the constitutional and institutional tools given to the Senate majority leader are much weaker than those wielded by the Speaker of the House.

Like the House, Senate leadership also includes party whips, formally titled assistant majority leader and assistant minority leader, but commonly referred to as majority or minority whip. Much like the whips in the House, these senators are charged with keeping track of votes and positions in their respective caucuses and, when necessary, persuading senators to support the leadership's positions.

The leadership includes others such as officers of the Democratic Conference, the Democratic Policy and Communications Committee, the Democratic Senatorial Campaign Committee (DSCC), the Republican Conference, the Republican Policy Committee, and the National Republican Senatorial Committee (NRSC).

The number of senators serving in the leadership in the Senate has gradually increased over recent decades, reflecting an effort by the parties to be more inclusive of factions and to ensure regional concerns are represented.

H. Congressional Committees

The crafting of legislation and the exercise of congressional oversight generally occurs in committees of the House and the Senate. For this reason, to influence policy legislation important to their constituencies, members seek positions on the committees with jurisdiction over such legislation. Party leaders and rules control members' assignment to committees and leadership of subcommittees, and the committees themselves have additional internal rules and procedures for assigning members to subcommittees.

Securing assignments to committees with jurisdiction over issues important to their constituencies is even more important in the House, where rank-and-file members have little opportunity to shape or amend legislation on the floor, as is more common in the Senate. These processes and decisions are important for personal office staff and advocates to understand, particularly at the outset of a new Congress, when the assignment process can take several weeks of negotiation.

Committees hold hearings taking testimony from administration officials, outside experts, interested stakeholders, and sometimes other members of Congress.

Congress has several types of committees, and they vary in the scope of their authority. They all draw their authority and jurisdiction from their respective chamber's rules. Standing committees persist from one Congress to the next, and form the majority of the legislative committees in both the House and Senate. Select committees (known in the Senate as select or special committees) have more narrow purposes, and are not necessarily permanent. Some select committees typically persist and are treated more like standing committees, such as the Intelligence Committees.

Majority leadership exerts control over the membership. The Speaker is empowered to unilaterally remove minority party members (as Speaker Kevin McCarthy did to members of the House Permanent Select Committee on Intelligence), or to deny them seats in the first place (as Speaker Nancy Pelosi did for prospective members of the Select Committee to Investigate the January 6th [2021] Attack on the United States Capitol). Joint committees have members from both the Senate and the House, but do not have legislative jurisdiction.

Members are appointed to House committees by the respective Republican and Democratic Steering Committees. Party leadership in each chamber makes recommendations, which are generally adhered to, although contested races are not unheard of. Once a nomination is made, formal approval is granted first by the party caucuses and then the full House or Senate by the adoption of resolutions ratifying the choices made by each party. Normally, these approvals are virtually automatic.

The overall size of committees and the party ratios of seats on committees are negotiated between the party leaderships. In the Senate, the expectation is that the ratio of committee seats assigned to majority and minority party members will reflect the party ratio in the full chamber. In the House, the majority party has much greater control. As a result, the most powerful committees are often more heavily weighted in favor of the majority. The Rules Committee, in particular, typically has a two-to-one ratio favoring the majority, plus an additional majority member. The Ways and Means Committee also typically has a lopsided majority to protect control over tax policy.

Committee work plays a crucial role in the legislative process. Because of this role, the act of stripping committee assignments from members is considered a serious sanction. Effective legislative strategy depends on understanding the motivations of members and senators to serve on particular committees, and appreciating how committees work with and against one another in the legislative process.

'

Chapter 2
Introduction of Legislation

Table of Sections

A. Introduction

In Article I, Section 1, the Constitution places the power and responsibility to legislate in the hands of Congress. It established a bicameral Congress in which neither body is able to make laws alone. The Founders designed Congress with two distinctly different chambers, and the histories of the House and Senate since 1787 has deepened those differences. At the same time, the difficulty of passing legislation and getting it to the president's desk has increased. Turning legislation into law requires steering it through first one chamber, then the other, and then resolving differences between them.

For legislation to become law, a bill must be passed by both the Senate and the House in exactly the same form—there cannot be the slightest difference in wording or punctuation—and presented to the president for signature or veto. This constitutional requirement is called "bicameralism and presentment." Because House members are responsible to 435 separate constituencies and senators represent fifty different states, passing legislation requires consideration and balancing of numerous interests shaped by party considerations, local issues, regional concerns, outside organizations, and other political factors.

In any case, the process begins with the drafting and submission of bills—that is, legislative measures.

B. Why Submit Legislation?

Historically, less than three percent of the thousands of bills introduced in each Congress actually become law. Some bills are written to address a problem or issue in which the member has a particular interest or expertise. The author may chair a committee or subcommittee that has legislative jurisdiction over a matter. At other times, bills may be introduced merely to raise an issue, stimulate debate, or set down a marker for future action. Some legislation is filed over and over for a number of years before progress or enactment occurs. Legislators may file a broad bill in the hope that a portion may eventually be incorporated into other legislation. Often, legislation is offered simply to demonstrate to constituents or interested groups that a member is committed to action on a particular matter; these are "messaging bills." Many of these bills never progress past the pro forma referral to a committee.

Legislation—and even legislative proposals—can have a meaningful effect on executive branch actions. Intense interest in a matter, whether demonstrated by groups of members or an individual member, can influence decisions even if the draft language never becomes law. The Department of Defense, for example, pays close attention to draft legislation from members of the Armed Services Committee in the House or the Senate.

Legislation referred to committees is in effect divided into three categories: bills that have no chance of being considered by the committee; bills that are not controversial and likely to be passed easily; and major bills that will require most of the committee's time. Most bills fall into the first category and are rarely the subject of committee hearings or formal consideration.

Both the Senate and the House permit the introduction of legislation "by request," meaning a third party has asked that the legislation be offered. A member of Congress may submit such a bill whether or not they support it. This might be done by leadership at the president's request, or by a committee or subcommittee chair on behalf of a department or government agency within their jurisdiction. For instance, the annual defense authorization act typically begins in the House with the introduction of a "by request" bill that reproduces the Defense Department's own set of legislative proposals for a given year. That version of the bill bears little resemblance to the final version of the bill. Individual members may also offer legislation requested by a constituent or an interest group. The designation "by request" is actually printed on the face of such legislation. This designation has no procedural effect on the consideration of that legislation.

Members sometimes introduce private bills that apply to one or several specific individuals. Most commonly, these bills concern immigration matters or claims against the U.S. government. The House lists such bills on the Private Calendar. The Senate, by contrast, does not distinguish private bills from public bills in terms of the procedure for consideration. Most private bills introduced never receive consideration on the House or Senate floor. Those that do may require subsequent introduction in more than one Congress to reach enactment. However, the fact that most private bills do not become law does not mean they are without impact. For example, the introduction of a private bill, alone, can freeze immigration proceedings in some circumstances.

In the first days of a new Congress, hundreds of bills are introduced—most of them reintroductions of legislation that failed to pass the prior Congress. All legislation not otherwise disposed of dies at the end of a Congress. However, legislation carries over between the *sessions* of a Congress if not enacted or disposed of.

In most cases, for legislation to gain traction in Congress—attracting the attention of party or committee leadership, finding its way to the floor of either chamber, surviving the legislative process, and ultimately being enacted—its sponsors must build momentum outside of Congress among the public, influential leaders of special interest groups, businesses, labor unions, sometimes academics, and other stakeholders. The media frequently plays a role in focusing attention on particular problems and emerging solutions.

C. Forms of Legislation

There are four general forms of legislation, each serving a specific purpose. The appropriate form depends on that purpose. These forms of legislation are the same in both chambers. Although legislative vehicles are frequently all referred to by the media and many others as a "bill," the legislative vehicle may be a *bill*, a *joint resolution*, a *concurrent resolution*, or a simple *resolution*.

D. Bills

Most legislation is drafted in the form of a bill. Bills can be narrowly drafted to address a discreet issue, or they can be extensive and address a multitude of issues. Most bills, in both chambers, are referred to one or more committees with jurisdiction over the issues that the bill addresses.

A bill passed in the same form in both chambers and signed by the president becomes law. The Constitution also provides two additional ways for a bill to become law without the president's signature. If the president does not act to sign (or veto) a bill within ten days (calendar days, not counting Sundays), it becomes law without the president's signature, *unless* the Congress has adjourned during that period. That latter outcome is referred to as the "pocket veto." The second way for a bill to become law without the president's signature is if each house votes to override the president's veto by a two-thirds majority.

Bills are numbered in the order in which they are introduced in each chamber: with an "H.R." designation in the House (e.g., H.R. 1) and an "S." in the Senate (e.g., S. 1). Chamber leadership typically reserves early numbers for bills that have exceptional political value.

Among the purposes of bills are to:

- authorize or prohibit certain government activities (authorization bills);
- appropriate funds out of the federal treasury (appropriations bills);
- amend the tax code (tax bills);
- amend existing federal laws; and
- provide various private relief to individuals (uncommon outside the immigration context).

E. Joint Resolutions

A joint resolution is similar to a bill, though it is usually narrower in scope. Like a bill, joint resolutions must be passed by both chambers. If passed in identical form and signed by the president—or allowed to become law without his signature, or passed over his veto—it becomes law.

The exceptions are joint resolutions proposing amendments to the Constitution (Article V), which are not presented to the president for signature, but rather go through a complex ratification process. Unlike bills, resolutions may contain a number of "whereas" clauses that detail the rationale for the resolution.

Joint resolutions are also numbered in a similar fashion to bills. In the House, they are designated as "H.J. Res." (e.g. H.J. Res. 1). In the Senate, joint resolutions are assigned "S.J. Res." numbers (e.g. S.J. Res. 1).

Among the uses for joint resolutions are:

- providing continuing appropriations (known as a continuing resolution or "CR");
- declaring war;
- approving or disapproving a presidential action or recommendation (e.g., under the Congressional Review Act or the War Powers Act); and
- addressing specific purposes, such as establishing a national holiday.

F. Concurrent Resolutions

Concurrent resolutions, in order to take force, must be adopted by both chambers with identical language. However, they do *not* go to the president and do *not* become law.

Concurrent resolutions are expressions of the will of Congress. In fact, some concurrent resolutions express the "sense of Congress" on an issue: the resolution states "It is the sense of the Congress that..." and lists one or more expressed opinions. Concurrent resolutions have been used to express Congress's views on a broad range of matters. For example, both the House and Senate adopted a concurrent resolution in 2013 expressing the view of Congress that North Korea should respect the fundamental human rights of its citizens and abandon, dismantle its nuclear weapons program, and end its nuclear and missile proliferation.

Although concurrent resolutions do not carry the force of law, they are influential and important. Resolutions provide the opportunity for members to show support or opposition to a policy without the need to pass a law. Government agencies, states, and foreign governments pay attention to how Congress is voting on issues of importance to them.

Concurrent resolutions are also used to take joint administrative actions. They are not binding except on Congress itself, which is subject to change by a later Congress. The most prominent concurrent resolution is the congressional budget resolution under the Budget and Impoundment Control Act of 1974.

Under Article I, Section 5, neither chamber can adjourn for more than three days without the approval of the other chamber. This approval is granted by means of a concurrent resolution, either for adjournment *sine die* (Latin for "without day") or other adjournments longer than the three-day limit.

Among the purposes for which concurrent resolutions are used are:

- enacting the congressional budget resolution;
- adjourning Congress;
- correcting enrolled measures;
- creating joint committees;
- providing for a joint meeting or session of Congress; and
- expressing the sense of Congress on some matter.

Concurrent resolutions, like bills and joint resolutions, are assigned a number as they are submitted and designated as "S.Con.Res." (e.g., S.Con. Res. 14) or "H.Con.Res" (e.g., H.Con.Res. 14).

G. Simple Resolutions

Simple resolutions may be adopted by either the Senate or the House. They are similar to concurrent resolutions in that they do not become law. They require adoption in only one chamber and are binding only on that chamber.

They are numbered sequentially and separately like bills, joint resolutions and concurrent resolutions. They are designed as "H.Res." in the House (e.g., H.Res. 14) and "S.Res." in the Senate (e.g., S.Res. 14).

Both the House and the Senate adopt "sense of the House" or "sense of the Senate" resolutions respectively to express the opinion of that body.

Simple resolutions are also used in each chamber to change the rules. In the House, this requires only a simple majority vote. In the Senate, although the rules may be changed by a simple majority, ending debate on a proposed change, in the event of a filibuster, may require a two-thirds vote of all senators voting provided a quorum of at least 51 senators is established. This makes it more difficult to adopt a controversial rules change.

In the House, simple resolutions reported by the Rules Committee play a crucial role and are an important tool for majority control (and the Speaker's power) in that chamber. For most major legislation, it is the Rules Committee that decides if and how a measure will be considered on the House floor.

Before a bill comes to the House floor for consideration, the Rules Committee reports a special rule in the form of a simple resolution to govern floor debate. Through this special rule, the committee determines whether any amendments are in order and if so, how many, and sometimes which specific amendments may be considered. The special rule also sets the time for debate, when the vote will occur, and under what procedures.

The house votes on the special rule in the form of a simple resolution before taking up the underlying legislation. These rule votes are typically along party lines, though a member's vote on the rule does not necessarily indicate how they will vote on the bill itself. For instance, a member of a minority party may have leverage by withholding a vote on the rule, even if they intend to vote for the substantive bill. Defeat of a rule is considered a major embarrassment for the majority leadership.

Some of the uses of a simple resolution include:

- changes to chamber rules;

- administration of the chamber;

- resolution of election contests;

- election of House or Senate officers;

- election of committee members;

- sense of the House or Senate on some matter; and

- in the House, special rules from the Rules Committee.

H. Sponsorship and Co-sponsorship

The member or senator who introduces legislation is known as the sponsor. Other members may wish to be closely identified with the introduction of a particular bill and sign on as cosponsors. Legislation can have numerous cosponsors.

Those who sign on before a bill is introduced are often referred to as "original cosponsors." This status may indicate more involvement (and a larger role in the actual drafting) than that of cosponsors who join after a bill is introduced.

Frequently, sponsors and other key proponents of legislation send a letter—known as a "Dear Colleague" letter—to other members explaining the purposes of the bill or resolution and seeking additional cosponsors. This practice is more common in the House because it is an efficient way to communicate a bill's intent to a large number of House members and to the public, but it is also seen in the Senate. However, because the Senate is a much smaller body, it is easier to seek the support of potential cosponsors directly. A bill's sponsor may also encourage supportive organizations and lobbyists outside of Congress to encourage other members to cosponsor. Dear Colleague letters are also used by members to communicate with all other members for many purposes beyond seeking cosponsorship.

I. Submitting Legislation

The formal submission of standalone legislation in the House traditionally begins when a member of Congress drops a copy of the bill or resolution signed by the sponsor into the "hopper," a mahogany wooden box located on the House floor, affixed to the side of the clerk's desk on the rostrum. In recent years, this process has migrated online, with electronic submissions now made through the "eHopper."

In the Senate, bills and resolutions are submitted by bringing a signed copy to the parliamentarian at the rostrum, located at the front of the chamber just below the presiding officer. Alternatively, the senator may submit the amendment by introducing the bill or resolution from the Senate floor. In the latter case, once the measure is introduced the presiding officer will state, "the bill will be received and appropriately referred."

Once the bill is submitted, it is assigned a number by the bill clerk reflecting the order in which bills were submitted in that particular Congress. In the House, the number will be preceded by "H.R." (e.g. H.R. 56), indicating the bill originated in the House. A bill introduced in the Senate will have an "S." designation (e.g. S. 56).

It has become customary for the majority leadership in each chamber to reserve the first several bill numbers—generally ten—for legislation reflecting the party's major policy priorities. Similarly, the next ten numbers are often reserved for use by the minority leadership. Members may also request specific bill numbers that carry symbolic value or are associated with legislation they have introduced in previous Congresses. Reusing a familiar bill number can make the measure more recognizable and help build momentum across years.

Identical bills may be introduced in both chambers. In committee sessions known as "markups," members may submit amendments to underlying legislation—often mirroring provisions found in standalone bills. The timing and substance of these amendments are governed by each committee's rules and procedures.

In both chambers, legislation can be introduced without any accompanying statement from the sponsor. In the House, there is usually no statement of introduction. In the Senate, it is common for a senator to submit a statement of introduction to appear in the *Congressional Record*, and on occasion, to deliver that statement on the Senate floor at the time of introduction.

Members in both chambers typically issue press releases announcing the introduction of legislation. For significant legislation, they may also hold news conferences or other events.

J. Referral to Committee

In both chambers, once introduced, most bills are referred to the appropriate standing committee with jurisdiction over the subject of the legislation. Similar to an original bill, legislation passed by one chamber is sent—or "messaged"—to the other body and is referred to a committee. Rules (principally Rule XXV in the Senate and Rule X in the House) and precedents have established jurisdictions for each chamber's committees. In some cases, the jurisdiction is affected by agreements made between committees. Such agreements are generally in writing in the form of a memorandum of understanding between the committees involved, which is subsequently placed in the *Congressional Record*. However, in the Senate, for the parliamentarian to act on such an agreement, a unanimous consent agreement is required to give it procedural force.

Legislative jurisdictions are vigorously defended by committees in both the House and Senate. Challenges to jurisdiction are usually negotiated between committee chairs and may lead to written agreements and unanimous consent agreements. On occasion jurisdictional battles spill onto the floor.

In the House, the Speaker determines which committee a bill is referred to. In the Senate, the presiding officer makes that determination pursuant to Senate Rule XVII and Rule XXV. In both chambers, the judgment is made by the respective parliamentarian and reliably followed by the presiding officer.

Committees with significant legislative drafting responsibilities will often ask their internal general counsel teams to make informal assessments about potential jurisdictional claims on provisions or amendments, even without the formal imprimatur of the parliamentarian. These internal reviews can preempt complications in the consideration and passage of a bill.

Most referral decisions are routine, but in some cases, overlapping jurisdictions or the complexity of a bill's text can make the committee referral difficult, and occasionally controversial.

The success or failure of a bill or resolution at the committee stage can depend greatly on its committee referral. Some committees might be more amenable to a particular proposal than others. Sometimes the fate of a measure can hinge on who chairs the committee.

As a result, bills are sometimes drafted with the committee referral in mind, using specific language that may influence the referral decision. The parliamentarian may advise sponsors on the factors used to determine jurisdiction and assist staff in crafting the strongest arguments to steer a bill to a specific committee.

When legislation impacts matters in the jurisdiction of several committees, it may be referred to more than one standing committee. This occurs more commonly in the House than in the Senate, where it almost always requires unanimous consent.

In the House, multiple referrals can take several forms. One committee is designated as the "lead" committee, while another may receive a "sequential" or "split" referral. A sequential referral refers to a circumstance in which a second committee considers the measure after it is reported by the lead committee. The Speaker may in such cases impose a time limit on the second committee's consideration. Also possible but less often used is a split referral. A split referral involves designating different segments of the bill to the lead and second committees.

In practice, "sequential referral" is a substantial impediment to legislation, at least at the committee stage. The secondary committee may not have the same incentives to legislate as the primary committee, or may have substantive or procedural objections to clearing the legislation. Accordingly, members and advocates should draft legislation carefully to avoid language that unintentionally triggers jurisdiction of a second (or successive) committee, assuming their goal is enactment of the legislation.

Once legislation reaches the House floor, the Rules Committee can and frequently does waive jurisdictional points of order against the bill, allowing a broader range of amendments to ride on the underlying bill. "Must-pass" measures like the annual National Defense Authorization Act thus become vehicles by which other authorization bills are passed. Critics deride this practice as turning the bill into a "Christmas tree" loaded with unsightly "ornaments"; proponents note the advantages of garnering support from members who may be more likely to vote for the underlying bill if ancillary issues are enacted as part of it.

In the Senate, the parliamentarian normally determines which committee's jurisdiction "predominates," and the legislation is referred to that committee in the name of the presiding officer. One common exception is the annual Intelligence Authorization Act, which is reported by the Senate Select Committee on Intelligence. The Senate Armed Service Committee routinely seeks and is granted sequential referral of this bill. This is because many of the personnel decisions and much of the funding provided for intelligence activities relate to parts of the Department of Defense.

K. Senate Rule XIV

Any senator may—and the majority leader frequently does—make use of Senate Rule XIV to bypass the normal referral of a bill or joint resolution to a standing committee. Under this rule, any senator can take steps to have the legislation placed directly on the Senate Calendar of Business on the next legislative day, making it available for floor consideration without committee action.

Senate Rule XIV requires that every bill or resolution submitted be read twice before being referred to committee. A third reading is required just prior to the vote on final passage. Rule XIV stipulates after the first two readings, "if objection be made to further proceeding thereon, [it shall] be placed on the Calendar." Because any senator may lodge such an objection, all senators have the procedural ability to circumvent the committee referral process and move legislation directly to the calendar, meaning that it is available for consideration on the Senate floor. This process takes two legislative days: the first when the measure is introduced and read twice, and the second after the Senate adjourns and then reconvenes. Since "legislative days" in the Senate do not correspond to calendar days—and only end when the Senate adjourns—this process may unfold over multiple calendar days.

However, getting legislation to the Senate's calendar by no means assures that it will be considered on the floor.

By Senate tradition and precedent, only the majority leader decides which matters will be scheduled for floor consideration. Therefore, as a practical matter, using Rule XIV as a strategy to bring a bill to the Senate floor without committee consideration is available only to the majority leader. It has been a powerful tool for the majority leader to expedite certain major legislation, to consolidate the work of several committees in one bill, or on occasion, to avoid the referral of the bill to a particular committee where the chair might have views different from those of the leadership.

L. Regular Order

In both chambers, some members have spoken out against the growing trend toward use of the rules to bypass what is commonly called "regular order." By this, members of Congress generally mean adherence to the normal legislative procedures set out in rules and precedents. Such procedures include the referral of legislation introduced to the committees of jurisdiction, public availability of proposed legislation, committee hearings, debate and consideration of amendments in committee mark ups, and the reporting of bills to the House or Senate floor for further debate and amendment.

Since the 1990s the regular order has not been respected on some pieces of major legislation. Bills crafted in the Speaker's office or the Senate majority leader's office have been brought directly to the floor through the Speaker's control of the House Rules Committee or the use of Rule XIV in the Senate.

The abandonment of regular order can be best illustrated with respect to the appropriations process. Congressional decisions about the expenditure of public funds, i.e., appropriations, normally require that the Appropriations Committee report separate appropriations bills that fund the various departments and agencies of government. However, Congress has increasingly failed to pass the necessary appropriations bills as required by the end of the fiscal year on September 30, risking a shutdown of the federal government. This has led lawmakers to rely on short-term joint resolutions known as "continuing resolutions" or huge "omnibus appropriations bills." Omnibus bills lump multiple appropriations measures together, sometimes with other extraneous legislation. These omnibus bills are sometimes sent directly to the House and Senate floors and passed, frequently with only minimal time for members to review their contents. If an omnibus only includes a few bills, maybe three or four, it may be referred to as a "minibus."

This popular use of the term "regular order" could confuse some observers of the Senate, since the term does have a technical parliamentary meaning in that body. In formal Senate procedure, it refers to returning to an amendment or measure set aside for another amendment or measure by unanimous consent, upon "a call for the regular order."

Chapter 3
Committees

A. Introduction

Much of the work of Congress occurs in committees. When each chamber follows its routine procedures, the vast majority of issues regarding any piece of proposed law are addressed at the committee stage of the legislative process. Pursuant to these routine procedures, it is in congressional committees that legislation is evaluated, debated, amended, shaped and, for most bills and resolutions, discarded.

Committee assignments are the primary way members of Congress engage with legislation. Many seek assignment to particular committees based on the subject-matter expertise they bring with them to Congress. Others use their positions on committees to develop specialized expertise. It is also common for members to pursue assignments to committees that oversee issues of particular importance to their constituents.

Committee assignments are especially important in the House. Rank-and-file House members—especially junior members or ones in competitive political districts—must develop areas of specialization with which they can serve their constituents. Committee assignments provide members with issues where they have the opportunity to play a significant role. For this reason, a vote to strip a member of his or her committee assignments is considered a serious form of censure.

Thousands of bills are introduced in each Congress. One of the first tasks of a committee in either chamber is to decide which of the hundreds of bills referred to them will receive actual consideration. Bills and resolutions generally fall into three categories: (1) those with no chance of passage, which will not be considered by the committee; (2) noncontroversial measures that will take little of the committee's time and energy and can likely be expedited; and (3) major legislation on which the committee will focus.

When a committee decides to take up a major bill, the decision is made primarily by the chair, who has wide discretion in setting the committee's agenda. Chairs frequently coordinate with chamber leadership on bills that are a priority for the majority party. At the same time, they must be mindful of the need to assemble a majority of the votes in the committee in order to report a bill to the floor. This often leads them to consult with other committee members, certainly members in the majority, but often with members in the minority as well.

B. Committees and Subcommittees

There are three types of committees in each chamber of Congress.

Standing committees in the Senate and House are permanent and have a defined legislative jurisdiction under Senate Rule XXV and House Rule X, respectively.

The second type of committee includes select or special committees, which are often temporary and created for a specific purpose. Some have legislative authority, some do not. The Senate has four such committees: Indian Affairs (which became a permanent committee in 1984); Ethics; Intelligence; and Aging. The Senate Indian Affairs and Intelligence Committees have legislative jurisdiction, the Senate Select Committee on Ethics and the Special Committee on Aging do not. In the House, the most notable is the Permanent Select Committee on Intelligence, which has legislative jurisdiction.

The third type of committee is a joint congressional committee, composed of members from each chamber. Established by law or concurrent resolution, joint committees have legislative information-gathering or administrative functions. Unlike standing committees or some select committees, joint committees have no legislative jurisdiction. There are currently four such committees: the Joint Committee on Taxation, the Joint Economic Committee, the Joint Committee on the Library, and the Joint Committee on Printing.

Each congressional committee creates its own rules consistent with guidelines contained in the rules of the House or Senate. Senate Rule XXVI establishes specific requirements for committees, including that the committee rules "not [be] inconsistent with the Rules of the Senate." Similarly, House Rule XI states that committee rules "may not be inconsistent with the Rules of the House." House Rule XI also states that the rules of the House "are the rules of its committees and subcommittees so far as applicable."

Committee rules address how oversight and hearings will proceed, how investigative subpoenas may be authorized and issued, and what authority resides with subcommittees. As such, a committee's rules determine the amount of influence that the chair, the minority, and individual members have over committee business.

Funding for committees is mostly provided through the annual Legislative Branch Appropriations bill. The distribution of those funds is controlled by biennial House and Senate resolutions, respectively.

With respect to funding, House Rule X stipulates only that the minority party be "treated fairly" (House Rule X, 6(d)). In recent Congresses, the Speaker has encouraged committee chairs to provide the minority with one-third of the funding. In practice, this ratio affects professional staff allocations and assignments; when partisan control of a committee changes hands, the outgoing majority staff is reduced in size by half, and incoming majority staff doubles. A small number of staff members may remain on the majority staff regardless of partisan control.

Senate rules, by contrast, establish no standard for the disbursement of committee funds to the majority and minority. In recent Congresses, the majority and minority leaders of the Senate have agreed to a funding formula, ratified by the adoption of a Senate resolution, based on the party division in the Senate, with additional funds allocated to the majority for the committee's administrative costs. In addition, the agreement has included the caveat that the minority cannot receive less than 40 percent of the full committee funding.

Because Senate rules protect the minority, fairness is policed by the minority party's potential ability to filibuster the funding resolution. The power of the filibuster in this respect was on display at the outset of the 107th

Congress. The 2000 election had resulted in a fifty-fifty split of Republicans and Democrats in the Senate. With the deciding vote of Republican Vice President Dick Cheney, the Republicans became the majority party in the 107th Congress. The minority, led by Minority Leader Tom Daschle (D-SD), threatened to filibuster unless a "power-sharing agreement" could be reached. Such an agreement was negotiated between Daschle and Majority Leader Trent Lott (R-MS). Among its provisions was that committee seats would be equally divided between members of each party on all committees and that committee budgets would be evenly split.

Committee staff tend to be seasoned professionals and subject-matter experts. They are typically known as "professional staff members" or "PSMs." PSMs with law degrees—regardless of whether they practice law in their committee role—are generally titled "Counsel." Staffing arrangements vary widely across committees. Staff positions are divided between the majority and minority parties. In some committees, the chair and ranking minority member of the full committee retain tight control over the staffing decisions for their respective parties. In other committees, subcommittee chairs may participate in the naming of committee staff, particularly those assigned to work with the subcommittees. For example, on the Senate Armed Services Committee, all staff decisions are traditionally made by the chair and the ranking minority member. Conversely, on the Homeland Security and Governmental Affairs Committee, subcommittee chairs hire their own staff.

Subcommittees are created by the committees as a means of dividing the workload and as a way of providing leadership roles (subcommittee chairs) for a broader range of members. Their use grew after 1946, when the committee system was reorganized and the number of standing committees in each chamber was reduced.

Subcommittee assignments are made by each committee from among its members. The role played by subcommittees differs depending on what they are tasked with doing by the full committee. Their activities can range from holding initial hearings on a policy or legislative idea to marking up and reporting bills to the full committee for its consideration.

Subcommittees play critical legislative roles in the House and Senate Appropriations Committees. Each appropriations subcommittee is responsible for drafting one of the appropriations bills required to fund the government each year. These subcommittees conduct extensive oversight of the administration's budget request, draft an appropriations bill with accompanying funding tables for the agencies in their jurisdiction, and mark up the bill before reporting it to the full committee. The choices made by the subcommittees are influential. It is not uncommon for the full House or Senate Appropriations Committee to mark up and report an appropriations measure prepared for it by a subcommittee without making any material changes.

For outside advocates, the importance of the subcommittee process means that engagement must begin early. In appropriations, many critical funding actions appear not in the actual legislative text of the bill, but rather in the accompanying report. The report language is customarily incorporated by reference into the bill text, giving it the force of law. The reports contain granular funding recommendations from the subcommittee that, barring unusual changes in the full committee or on the House floor, will represent the House position in conference negotiations with the Senate.

Typically, an appropriations report describes funding by reference to the president's annual budget submission. For a particular item, the subcommittee will explain increases or decreases with short descriptions of the justification. These descriptions are commonly known as "stub entries," and give brief rationale for the deviation. Advocates and staff members must read, understand, and analyze report language carefully to design and execute effective appropriations strategies.

On other committees, the major work and consideration of legislation is retained at the full committee level. Several committees conduct hearings in the subcommittee and then mark up bills (that is, consider amendments) in the full committee. In the House Armed Services Committee, for instance, subcommittee markups are pro forma sessions completed in mere minutes. The full committee markup, by contrast, frequently lasts more than ten hours and features debate on hundreds of amendments.

The power and independence of a subcommittee depend in large part on the latitude provided to subcommittee chairs within a committee to select and supervise subcommittee staff and manage the budget for that staff. The degree of control excercised by the full committee chair over the hiring, firing, and supervision of subcommittee staff varies greatly from committee to committee.

When a bill is referred to a committee, if the committee decides to act, that bill is sometimes held at the full committee level for legislative action. Most commonly, however, bills are referred to the appropriate subcommittee of jurisdiction where hearings will take place. At the conclusion of the hearings, the subcommittee may act on the measure—that is, mark up the bill and report it to the full committee. In some instances, following hearings, a measure may be returned to the full committee for debate and amendment. Whatever action is taken by the subcommittee, the committee chair may decide to repeat the step in the full committee, or the committee may simply act to report the subcommittee's product to the House or Senate floor.

C. Committee Chairs

Congressional committee chairs are very powerful. During periods when the centralized leadership of the House or Senate is weak, the role of committee chairs becomes even more powerful.

The majority member who has served on the committee the longest is frequently named as the chair. This is known as the "seniority system." For much of congressional history, the seniority system was nearly ironclad.

However, in recent decades, Speakers and the respective steering committees in the House have increasingly named chairs who are not the senior-most members of the majority on the committee.

By contrast, in the Senate, decisions by the two parties in choosing chairs and ranking minority members of the various committees are ratified by a vote of the Senate on the so-called committee organizing resolutions. The

Senate has largely continued to follow the seniority system for the selection of chairs, with some exceptions. However, in the 1970s both parties decided that seniority should not dictate the choice of committee chairs. In 1995, the Republicans changed rules to permit Republican members of the committee to vote for the chair without regard to seniority.

Because committee chairs exercise considerable discretion over committee action, contests for committee leadership can have high stakes. The chair presides over hearings, markups, and other committee meetings. The chair largely determines the committee agenda and controls most of the committee's staff and funding. In addition, the chair controls the referral of bills and resolutions to the subcommittees. Although the opposition of a committee chair to a bill or provision may be overcome, it is difficult.

The ranking member leads the minority party on the committee and may or may not be widely consulted by the chair, depending on the rules, the political climate, their personal relationship, and the duties of the committee. The ranking member controls a portion of the budget and names minority witnesses for hearings. Committees responsible for generating and shepherding "must-pass" legislation every year tend to have majority-minority relationships that are more collaborative. Especially in the Senate, some chairs and ranking members forge a close working relationship.

There are limits on the number of chair or ranking minority positions a member may hold on committees and subcommittees. Senate Rule XXV and both parties in the House impose these limitations. In practice, Senate ratios are as much a product of post-election negotiations between the parties as they are a reflection of the rote application of Rule XXV.

Senate Rule XXV divides Senate committees into three categories designated "A," "B," and "C." These are ranked by their relative importance, with "A" committees being the highest. These classifications are used to impose limitations on the number of assignments a senator may have in each. For example, senators are limited to membership on two Class A committees. These include most of the standing committees and the Select Committee on Intelligence. Waivers from these limitations are common.

The most coveted committee assignments are to the so-called "Super A" committees. Senators may only sit on one such committee. The Democrats consider the Appropriations Committee, the Finance Committee, and the Armed Services Committee to be "Super A" committees. The Republicans include the Foreign Relations Committee as a fourth "Super A" committee. The limitation on "Super A" committee assignments for any senator are sometimes also waived.

In 1995, House Republicans, under Speaker Newt Gingrich (R-GA), adopted term limits for committee chairs. In the House, Republicans may serve as chair or ranking minority member of a committee or subcommittee for no more than three consecutive terms—six years—with time spent as chair and as ranking minority member counting toward the limit. That same year, Senate Republicans also imposed term limits of six years as chair of a standing committee. However, a senator may serve a separate six years as ranking member of the same Senate committee. Neither House nor Senate Democrats impose term limits on committee or subcommittee chairs.

D. Hearings in Committees

Committees use hearings to conduct oversight and to inform legislation under consideration. In both chambers, committee hearings must be open to the public unless the committee, in open session, votes to close the hearing. The most common reason for closed hearings is to protect classified national security material or testimony. For example, many of the hearings held by the House and Senate Intelligence Committees are closed. Hearings are also sometimes closed for other reasons, such as to take witness testimony in an investigation. The public release of transcripts or information obtained in closed sessions requires a majority vote of the committee.

A witness may testify either individually or as a member of a panel. At times, a committee may require that a witness testify under oath. Witnesses may include executive branch officials, representatives of the private sector or public interest organizations, academics, and, occasionally, members of Congress who are not on the committee.

Committees generally require witnesses to file an advance written statement in the days preceding the hearing and limit their oral testimony to a brief summary. Private sector witnesses must also file "Truth in Testimony" disclosure forms listing their affiliations and government contracts, pursuant to House rules that are mirrored in committee rules. These forms are generally made public, except where publication would result in release of classified or controlled information.

Subsequent to the oral statements by witnesses, and sometimes opening statements by members of the committee, committee members question the witnesses. In the House, the rules of all committees require a five-minute limit for the first rounds of questions to witnesses. In the Senate, some committees have established a five-minute rule. Time limits on questions are often set by the chair, frequently in consultation with the ranking member. The chair can decide to allow additional rounds of questioning.

Members of the committee may also ask witnesses to respond to questions in writing at a later time. Members are also able to submit questions for the record ("QFRs"), which are written questions submitted for the hearing record that require written responses from witnesses. The chair will often permit the record to remain open for additional material to be submitted.

Committee hearings are sometimes sparsely attended by members of the committee. Since members serve on multiple committees and subcommittees, there are often scheduling conflicts they must juggle— particularly in the Senate.

Senate Rule XXVI authorizes committees to establish a quorum of as few as one-third of members to conduct routine committee business. Senate committee rules vary, but quorum requirements to hear testimony can be as few as one member. House Rule XI requires at least two members for a committee to take testimony. Even if committee members are unable to attend hearings, the member's staff will often be present in order to brief the member should they arrive late or to report back at a later time.

In addition to legislative hearings, committees regularly hold a range of other hearings. Oversight hearings support Congress's constitutional responsibility to assess how well programs are being carried out by the Executive Branch.

Confirmation hearings allow senators to question and evaluate executive or judicial nominees. Investigative hearings focus on matters within the committee's jurisdiction that may involve scandals, wrongdoing, or criminal behavior. Witnesses at investigative hearings may also be required to testify or provide written materials under subpoena.

Although most hearings are held in Washington, committees sometimes hold field hearings in locations related to the subject of the hearing or the home state or district of a committee member.

E. Markups

A committee or subcommittee may decide to hold a business meeting to take action on a measure after the hearings have concluded. One purpose of a business meeting is to debate and amend a measure. This is referred to as a "markup" session.

Like the rules for public hearings, both the House and Senate require that markups be open to the public unless the committee, by majority vote in open session, closes the markup.

A quorum of at least one-third of the committee members is required under the rules of both chambers in order to hold a markup session. Some committees establish a higher number. The vote to report the legislation requires a quorum of a majority of the committee.

Some committees in the Senate permit their members to vote by "proxy" during a markup. A proxy is a signed piece of paper stating the member's intent with respect to votes to be held in a markup session they are unable to attend. On occasion such proxies may be open ended and allow the chair or another committee member to cast the proxy vote for the absent senator. Sometimes a senator's staff will have been supplied with proxies for expected votes. The staffer may provide them to the chair as appropriate. Proxy voting is not permitted in the House.

The chair of the committee or subcommittee will likely decide what version of a piece of legislation will be used as the base text for the committee to mark up. This is referred to as the "chairman's mark." The selection of base text is an important power for the chair and can significantly influence the final product.

Provisions in the chair's mark may only be changed or deleted by majority vote during the markup process, a clear advantage for the chair. The chair's mark may be legislation that was introduced and referred to the committee or an entirely new alternative measure.

In some committees, when a subcommittee has marked up a bill and reported it to the full committee, that bill will serve as the vehicle for amendment. In such cases, the reported text is often printed or offered by the chair as a substitute for the original measure that was referred to the committee. The chair may also introduce an entirely new bill incorporating the subcommittee's changes; that measure is then referred back to the committee and used as the markup vehicle.

At the outset of the markup, the chair usually permits opening statements. The chair speaks first, followed by the ranking committee member. The remaining committee members present are then recognized in alternating order between the parties.

F. Amendment Procedure

The amendment procedure in committee markups generally follows the same rules as on the floor. Committees may modify some rules, but these modifications cannot be inconsistent with the rules of the chamber. In the Senate, the floor amendment process is largely governed by practices and precedents, but it is far less transparent in real time than the House floor process. The House Rules Committee publishes an online, publicly accessible, consolidated list of amendments submitted for consideration, and updates the outcomes shortly after Rules Committee members take votes. Although Senate amendments are published in the *Congressional Record*, the status and disposition are much more difficult for outside parties and non-committee members to track.

Bills and resolutions in committee may be amended in two degrees—that is, an amendment to the language, plus an amendment to that amendment, are in order. In the House, amendments must be germane, meaning they must pertain to the same subject as the legislation or amendment to which they are offered.

Amendments in committee may add new language, delete specific language from the bill, or both delete and replace language. At the end of the process, the committee reports the legislation—with any amendments adopted by the committee—to the floor.

House committees generally consider a bill section by section. When all amendments to one section have been considered, that section is closed to further amendment and the committee moves on to the next section. The chair may decide to allow amendment to any provision in the bill and this may be accomplished by unanimous consent. If a full substitute amendment is offered (only permitted at the beginning or end of the markup), that measure itself is open to amendment at any point.

Measures are usually open to amendment at any point in Senate committees. Germaneness is not required, but an amendment reported by a committee containing any significant matter outside of the committee's legislative jurisdiction is subject to a point of order if adopted in committee and considered on the Senate floor.

When an amendment is offered, it is read and copies are distributed. By unanimous consent, the committee may dispense with the reading of the amendment.

In the House, committee debate on amendments is generally limited by the five-minute rule, and may be reduced to smaller increments of time. Senate committee rules permit more extended debate, but committees have adopted rules that can curtail a filibuster of an amendment in committee.

Amendments in committee are adopted or rejected by majority vote. Votes are conducted by voice vote or roll call. On a voice vote, the chair will ask those voting in the affirmative to say "aye" and those opposed to say "nay." The chair judges which side prevailed, but members may request a recorded vote to document the outcome and establish how each member voted.

Members may offer an amendment that is controversial and expected to fail, and then withdraw the amendment before the vote is taken. "Offer and withdrawal" permits the member's amendment to be discussed without establishing a defeat in committee. In large markups, most amendments are noncontroversial, after careful coordination with member offices and majority and minority staff. Those amendments, which have been coordinated and agreed upon by the majority and minority, are bundled into "en bloc" packages of dozens or even hundreds and voted on as a single package. The en bloc process streamlines debate and reduces the chance of amendment or failure of any provision included in a package.

When all sections of the measure have been considered by a House committee, the "previous question" is moved. This is the parliamentary procedure that ends debate. If the previous question is adopted, it brings the measure to a final committee vote. This motion is not subject to debate.

G. Reporting Legislation to the Floor

At the end of the markup process, a motion is made to report the measure favorably to the House or Senate. A committee may also report a measure unfavorably or without recommendation. Legislation reported unfavorably or without recommendation by a committee is rare. This may occur if there is a statutory requirement to report a bill or if the committee believes that the full House or Senate should have the opportunity to work its will on a measure even though it's not supported by the committee.

In both the House and the Senate, a majority of committee members voting, with a quorum present, is needed to approve a measure and to report it to the chamber floor. Under House and Senate rules, a majority of the committee is necessary to establish the quorum. Some Senate committees permit voting by proxy on the motion to report a measure. However, under Senate rules, committees cannot permit proxies to affect the outcome of the vote to report the measure, meaning that a member's proxy will be recorded as long as it is not necessary to approve or defeat the measure. Under consistent interpretations of the Senate's rules, if a committee permits proxies on the vote to report a measure, only negative proxies count. Proxies also cannot be used to establish the necessary quorum to report a bill or resolution.

Committees report a bill to the full House or Senate with amendments or incorporate those amendments in an omnibus "amendment in the nature of a substitute." The chair may also decide to have the committee introduce an original bill, known as a "clean bill" in the House and an "original bill" in the Senate. This is a new bill, with a new number, reflecting all of the actions taken by the committee during markup. If many changes were made to the legislation during markup, reporting an original bill may facilitate floor action by avoiding separate consideration of each committee-adopted amendment.

Committees are not required to take any action on bills or resolutions referred to them, and the majority of bills and resolutions are not acted upon. Therefore, if a committee does not report a bill or resolution referred to it, the bill or resolution normally cannot be considered on the floor. In the Senate, it is possible to offer such legislation as an amendment on the floor. However, both chambers have rules providing a means of bringing a measure to the floor that has not been reported by a committee.

Under Senate rules, a motion to discharge a bill from a committee can be made by any senator, but absent unanimous consent, consideration of such a motion is almost impossible. If a discharge motion is agreed to—which requires a majority vote but is subject to filibuster—the measure is removed from the committee and placed on the Senate's Calendar of Business. Such motions in the Senate are rare, and are frowned upon by the majority leadership.

Senate Rule XIV permits any senator (usually the majority leader) to circumvent the normal referral of a measure to committee and allows that measure to be placed on the Senate Calendar of Business.

In the House, under Rule XV, any member may file a discharge petition with the Clerk of the House once the committee has had a measure for more than 30 days. A discharge petition must reference only one measure, not multiple pieces of legislation. While discharge petitions are sometimes threatened by the minority, success requires the petition to be signed by a majority of the House (normally 218 members) and is therefore exceedingly rare. Once the necessary signatures appear on a discharge petition, a motion to discharge is placed on the House's Discharge Calendar. Signatures remain valid even if the signing member resigns or dies.

Any member who signed the petition is eligible under the rules to offer the motion on the floor, although such motions are restricted to a "discharge day," which occurs only on the second and fourth Monday of each month. If a majority votes for the motion when it is brought up on discharge day, the measure is brought to the floor. Since the House is a majoritarian body, a successful discharge petition is rare, and considered a rebuke to the Speaker, the majority leadership, and the Rules Committee.

It may take a considerable period of time from the point at which a measure is reported to the House or Senate to when the decision is made by the House or Senate leadership to call it up for floor consideration. Many factors can influence that decision, including timelines for expiring authorization legislation, appropriations deadlines, politics and public opinion, available floor time, a pending recess, or any number of other considerations.

Legislation reported to the House floor is placed either on the Union Calendar, for bills that raise or spend funds, or the House Calendar, used for other measures. In the Senate, legislation is placed on the Legislative Calendar (Senate Calendar of Business).

H. Committee Reports

A committee report is a document drafted by the committee that explains a piece of legislation and any amendments adopted by the committee. The report often makes arguments for why the full chamber should accept the committee's recommendation on the legislation.

House Rule XIII requires committees to file a committee report. In the Senate, the filing of a committee report is at the discretion of the committee, but is common.

A committee report is written by the majority of the committee, frequently in collaboration with the minority. Members in opposition to the reported bill or resolution may choose to file minority views. At times, supplemental or additional views can also be included. Supplemental or additional views are typically filed by committee members who agree with the majority or the minority, but on different or additional grounds. These may be filed by individual members or groups of committee members to amplify issues addressed by the bill.

Committee reports are generally closed to amendment once they are voted on and reported out by a committee. This means that elements of report language may be subject to amendment during committee markups, but are usually not subject to amendment on the floor.

Committee reports can influence the debate and decisions in the full chamber. Committee reports may also be used by executive branch agencies and others to more fully understand the legislation. In litigation, judges may examine committee reports and floor debate records for evidence of the legislative history and congressional intent. However, judges may decline to give any weight to report language, holding that congressional intent is contained solely and entirely in the text of a statute that meets the elements of bicameralism and presentment.

Appropriations committees frequently give their subcommittees' reports the force of law by incorporating them into statutory text. For example, a House appropriations bill text may contain relatively high-level categories of appropriations, but its accompanying report may contain hundreds of pages of tables making precise directions and line-item funding provisions. A section of the bill text can incorporate these decisions with a catch-all provision:

> With regard to the list of specific programs, projects, and activities (and the dollar amounts and adjustment to budget activities corresponding to such programs, projects and activities) contained in the tables titled Explanation of Project Level Adjustments in the explanatory statement regarding this Act ... the obligation and expenditure of amounts appropriated or otherwise made available in this Act for those programs, projects, and activities are ***hereby required by law to be carried out in the manner provide by such tables to the same extent as if the tables were included in the text of this Act*** [emphasis added].

The report of a House-Senate appropriations conference, called a "joint explanatory statement," takes a similar approach to preserve and harmonize the requirements of report language incorporated by each chamber:

> Unless otherwise noted, the language set forth in House Report [Number] and Senate Report [Number] carry the same weight as language included in this joint explanatory statement and should be complied with unless specifically addressed to the contrary in this joint explanatory statement.

Members and advocates who work on appropriations provisions must pay close attention to report language for impacts to relevant programs, since those provisions carry binding legal impacts.

Other report language, while lacking the legal force of statutory text, is more influential than a mere exposition of congressional intent. Armed Services Committee reports contain hundreds of pieces of "directive report language" that instruct Defense Department leaders to take a certain action by a deadline, usually to provide a briefing or report to the committee on an issue within its legislative jurisdiction. Because report language lacks the force of law, it is unsuitable for spending direction or significant policy mandates, but it remains an important tool in congressional oversight of defense spending and operations.

Chapter 4
House Floor

Table of Sections

A. Introduction

While much of the work on legislation is done in committee, bills must pass the full chamber. Whether legislation successfully leaves the House floor depends heavily on the Speaker, majority leadership, and the Rules Committee.

Article I, Section 5 of the Constitution grants the House the power to write its own rules, including the parliamentary rules under which measures are considered. These rules are adopted by majority vote at the outset of each new Congress, often with slight alterations. In some Congresses, sweeping changes to the rules occur, especially when the speakership changes parties.

Understanding the differences in legislative procedures between the highly structured House of Representatives and the less predictable Senate is central to understanding lawmaking.

The House is a majoritarian body. This means that it is governed by majority vote. Thus, the Speaker, elected by that majority, wields great potential power, traditionally executed over legislation through the House Rules Committee.

The Speaker's power stems from the ability to hold the majority together or to forge a temporary coalition with the minority—often a difficult task. In extreme cases, an insurgent faction of the majority can join with the minority to offer a motion to "vacate the chair," deposing the Speaker. Only once has this tactic succeeded: in October 2023, Speaker Kevin McCarthy (R-CA) was removed after having agreed at the start of his speakership to a rules package that allowed a single member to introduce the motion to vacate. Eight of his fellow Republicans voted for the motion, and he was immediately stripped of his speakership, but not his status as a member of the House.

In the 113th Congress, Speaker John Boehner (R-OH) lost reliable control of the House Republican Conference. On some major legislation—most notably a continuing resolution to avoid a government shutdown—Speaker

Boehner was required to work with Minority Leader Nancy Pelosi (D-CA) to whip votes to pass legislation. In October 2013, the government shut down for sixteen days when Congress could not agree on appropriations for the new fiscal year. With public disapproval of the shutdown rising, Boehner negotiated compromise legislation to reopen the government. Eighty-seven Republicans supported the bill, alongside all 198 Democrats. However, Boehner's repeated reliace on the minority deepened tensions with the conservative wing of his majority party in the House, and he decided to step down as Speaker.

Normally, the Speaker—working with the rest of the majority leadership and the committee chairs—retains firm control over the legislative process in the House. Speakers often adhere to a practice formerly known as the "Hastert Rule," under which the Speaker will only bring a bill to the House floor for a vote if a *majority of the majority* supports it. Although not a formal rule of either the House or the party conference, this practice was closely associated with former Republican Speaker Dennis Hastert and has been followed by many Speakers after him. Few members now use his name for the practice following his 2016 conviction and imprisonment for financial crimes connected to child sex abuse.

Among the most powerful House Speakers was Thomas Brackett Reed, elected Speaker in 1889. As both Speaker and chair of the Rules Committee, Reed was the architect of an array of parliamentary changes—known as the "Reed Rules"—that greatly strengthened the office and established him as the first of the modern Speakers.

B. Scheduling of Legislation

Measures reported to the House from a committee are placed on a calendar. There are two main calendars on which bills and resolutions reported from committees are placed in the House: the Union Calendar and the House Calendar. Two others, less frequently used, are the Private Calendar and the Discharge Calendar.

All bills that spend funds or raise revenues are placed on the Union Calendar. Other reported legislation goes on the House Calendar, except for private bills, which are intended to affect an individual or group of individuals. Some private bills, for example, affect an individual's immigration status. Private relief measures are listed on the Private Calendar.

The Discharge Calendar is reserved for motions to discharge committees. Such motions are placed on the Discharge Calendar once a discharge petition has received the necessary number of signatures, which is a majority of the total membership of the House, normally 218.

The Speaker, majority leader, and other members of the majority leadership decide if and when legislation listed on any of the House calendars will receive floor consideration. Such decisions must be consistent with House Rules, which influence the priority of certain bills and dictate the specific days when a measure can normally be considered. Even when a measure appears on one of these calendars, there is no guarantee it will reach the House floor.

Much of the power wielded by modern Speakers and the majority leadership stems from their control of House scheduling. A speaker must weigh and balance numerous competing factors when making scheduling decisions. Pressures on the Speaker include the opinions and desires of the committee chairs, the views of the party caucus (including internal factions), the administration (particularly if the president is of the same party), outside interest groups, public opinion, and the Senate.

C. House Rules Committee

House leadership, working with the Rules Committee, controls how a measure is considered. The Speaker ensures that the ratio of majority to minority members on the Rules Committee is heavily weighted toward the majority—almost always at least a two-to-one advantage. The Speaker also typically appoints members loyal to the leadership, although political challenges during the 118th and 119th Congresses forced Republican

Speakers to add members from insurgent factions to the Committee.

In many ways, the Rules Committee is the most powerful committee in the House. It functions as the Speaker's strong arm because of its role in scheduling major legislation and dictating the process by which that legislation is considered. The committee can hold legislation without a hearing for a considerable period—or even indefinitely—to kill it, often at the Speaker's direction to avoid forcing the majority to take responsibility for a vote on an unpopular measure.

The Rules Committee exercises jurisdiction over the order of business in the House. For most major legislation, it determines if and how a measure will be considered on the floor. The committee will hold a hearing and take member testimony focused exclusively on the proposed bill or resolution, as well as potential amendments.

When a House committee reports legislation, its chair contacts the Rules Committee chair to request a hearing and a special rule. The Rules Committee chair typically holds a hearing only after the leadership has decided to schedule the measure for floor consideration. In consultation with the leadership, the chair usually decides when that hearing will be held.

Rules Committee hearings are similar to those held by other committees; however, only members of the House are generally invited to testify. The chair and ranking member of the committee that reported the measure under consideration typically testify before the Committee. The author of the bill or resolution, if different than the chair, may also testify, as may other members seeking support for a particular amendment.

D. Special Rules

When the hearing concludes, the Rules committee decides whether to grant a special rule for consideration of the measure. Under regular order, House Rule XVII provides for one hour of debate, equally divided between the parties. A special rule allows leadership to more tightly control proceedings on the floor. It takes the form of a simple House resolution (H.Res. ###) reported by the Rules Committee, which must be adopted by a majority vote of the House. If adopted, the resolution specifies what amendments, if any, will be in order and how much debate will be permitted before a vote on passage.

A "special rule" has that title because, for the purposes of the measure under consideration, it supersedes the general rules of the House. It is a privileged matter on the House floor, meaning it has priority over the regular order of business defined under House Rule XIV. In reality, the House rarely follows the regular order; most legislative business is overwhelmingly conducted either by unanimous consent or as privileged matters.

Special rules frequently dictate how a measure can be debated. For an amendment to be considered at all, the Rules Committee must vote to make it "in order." Special rules typically provide for a fixed period of general debate on the House floor and may stipulate whether debate will be allowed on amendments, and if so, how much time will be allotted for those amendments. In recent years, the Rules Committee has posted near-real-time access to amendments submitted and made in order. Although this transparency is helpful, staff and advocates must track the status of amendments—"submitted" amendments that are not "made in order" will simply die in the Rules Committee—and follow the changing numbering conventions for amendments at each stage of the Rules Committee and floor consideration.

A special rule can also determine what types of amendments and how many amendments, if any, may be offered to a measure on the floor. It may also waive all potential points of order against the bill, including jurisdictional points of order, allows for a broader scope of amendments than in the committee markup process.

If the special rule permits amendments on the floor without restriction, it is known as an "open rule." Under House Rule XVI, all amendments must be germane, meaning they must relate to the same subject as the bill under consideration. For much of the House's history, open rules were common.

As the House has become more polarized along partisan and ideological lines, open rules have become less popular with House leadership, because they can give rise to time-consuming and unpredictable debate and results. Tighter control of special rules can also prevent the minority from offering amendments that the majority does not wish to consider.

If a rule prevents floor amendments entirely, it is known as a "closed rule." Some rules—called "modified closed rules" or "modified open rules"— allow only limited amendments. The distinction between these two types of modified rules hinges on how restrictive the limitations are on floor amendments and is therefore somewhat subjective. A modified open rule may limit amendments to those printed in advance in the *Congressional Record*, place an overall limit on submission and debate of amendments, or both. Modified closed rules limit amendments to specific ones identified in the special rule.

E. Privileged Business

"Privileged" bills or resolutions are those that, under House Rules, can interrupt the regular order of business to be taken up, debated, and voted on. Matters privileged in the House include special rules from the Rules Committee, appropriations bills, budget resolutions, reconciliation bills, conference reports, and reports from the House Ethics Committee. Privileged business also includes legislation listed on certain calendars— such as the Private Calendar and the Discharge Calendar—which are privileged on certain dedicated days.

Motions to discharge, which have taken on prominence in closely divided Congresses, may be called up on the House floor as a privileged matter by any member who signed the discharge petition.

F. Motion to Suspend the Rules

Most legislation considered by the House is done so by suspending the rules (Rule XV). Bills and resolutions that are not controversial and are supported by a large majority of the members can pass under expedited procedures. Passage of a measure under suspension of the rules requires a two-thirds vote.

The Speaker may recognize a member to move to "suspend the rules and pass" a measure, which may occur only on Monday, Tuesday, or Wednesday of each week, unless by unanimous consent. On occasion, the motion will stipulate "suspend the rules and pass *with an amendment.*" In such cases, no separate vote on the amendment will occur on the House floor.

When the House considers a bill under suspension of the rules, amendments are not in order, debate is limited (usually to 40 minutes), and no points of order can be raised against the measure. If a recorded vote (two-thirds required) is not requested, such bills can often be passed by voice vote.

G. Debate

If the special rule is adopted, the House usually convenes as the "Committee of the Whole House on the State of the Union" to debate the measure. The Committee of the Whole, as it is commonly called, is made up of all House members. It is, in effect, the House of Representatives in a different parliamentary form. The House resolves into the Committee of the Whole either by special rule or by unanimous consent. A quorum of 100 members is required to conduct business in the Committee of the Whole. It is within the Committee of the Whole that the bill or resolution will be debated and any amendments considered.

When the House resolves itself into a Committee of the Whole, the Speaker or Speaker pro tempore steps down and appoints a chair to preside. The presiding member is addressed as "Mr. Chairman" or "Madam

Chairwoman," and not as "Mr. Speaker" or "Madam Speaker." The use of a committee composed of all members to consider controversial and often complex legislation dates back to the early years of the House.

As a symbol of the change from the House to the Committee of the Whole, the "mace" is moved. The mace is a 46-inch staff of ebony and silver, adopted by the first House in 1789, that signifies the dignity and authority of the chamber. Historically, the Sergeant at Arms has used it to restore order by parading it before offending members—reportedly last done during World War I. When the House meets, the mace rests on a pedestal on the rostrum to the right of the Speaker. When the Committee of the Whole meets, it moves the mace to a lower pedestal. Viewers watching the chamber on C-SPAN can identify which body is meeting by noting the mace's height on the left side of the screen.

H. Amendment on the House Floor

In the Committee of the Whole, as on the House floor, amendments must be germane—meaning they must be relevant to the bill or amendment to which they are offered and fall within the legislative jurisdiction of the reporting committee. The House germaneness rule is complex, with numerous precedents arising from its interpretation and application. If a point of order is raised that an amendment is not germane, the parliamentarian typically advises the Speaker or the chair of the Committee of the Whole on the proper ruling, and that advice is almost always followed.

If the special rule adopted is an open rule, any germane amendment that complies with House rules and the Budget Act may be offered. A special rule that permits amendments but imposes some limits on consideration is known as a "modified open rule." If the Rules Committee specifies a single amendment or a list of amendments and prohibits all others, the special rule is a "modified closed rule." Under a closed rule, no amendments are in order.

Amendments, even if otherwise in order, may be constrained by the "amendment tree." This is a diagram showing the types and number of amendments permitted to be pending in the House at any given time, as well as the order in which they may be offered and voted upon.

The base bill text forms the trunk of the amendment tree. An amendment to that base bill is a "first-degree" amendment. This proposed amendment may be altered by a "perfecting" amendment, which alters but does not completely replace the language, or by a "substitute," which strikes the proposed amendment and replaces it with new text. A first-degree amendment and a substitute can each be further amended in the "second degree."

When fully occupied, the House amendment tree can hold four amendments. If all four are pending, they are voted upon in the following order: (1) the second-degree perfecting amendment to the first-degree amendment to the bill text; (2) the second-degree perfecting amendment to the substitute amendment; (3) the substitute amendment, as amended if applicable by that second-degree vote; and (4) the first-degree amendment to the base bill.

As amendments—depicted as branches on the tree—are disposed of, that branch becomes open again for another amendment of the same type. However, no amendment may alter language that has already been amended.

I. Voting

Recorded votes by individual members in the House are displayed on a lighted scoreboard on the wall above the visitors' gallery, clearly visible from the floor. Members are able to quickly check the votes cast by others of their party in their state delegation, their committee chair, or others whose votes may provide guidance. In this way, if a member is inclined to vote in a certain way, but finds unexpected discordance with others they typically vote with, they may seek clarification before casting their vote. Members of each party's whip team are usually responsible for communicating the leadership position. On some votes, the leadership will decline to "whip," allowing members more leeway to vote according to their judgment or constituent interests, even if those votes diverge from party leadership's position.

There are four methods for counting votes on House floor: voice vote, yeas and nays, division (or "standing") vote, and record vote. Voice votes, division votes, and recorded votes are also used in the Committee of the Whole.

When voice votes are taken, members shout "yea" and "nay," and the presiding officer judges which side prevails. Once the voice vote is taken, any member may demand a division vote. In a division vote, those voting "yea" are asked to stand, followed by those voting "nay." The presiding officer counts and announces the totals, but individual votes are not recorded.

Both yeas and nays and record votes are taken by electronic device: members insert their voting card into a slot in one of many voting stations on the floor and press a button to indicate "yea," "nay," or "present." If a yeas and nays vote is taken, any member may object on the ground that a quorum is not present. Under those circumstances, the electronic vote will determine both the outcome of the vote and the establishment of a quorum. A "record vote" is taken when requested if one-fifth of a quorum in the House (44 members) or one-fourth of a quorum in the Committee of the Whole (25 members) rise in support of the request. The individual votes of members are displayed on the electronic scoreboard in the House chamber. Normally, the minimum time for a record vote, yeas and nays, or quorum call is fifteen minutes in both the House and the Committee of the Whole. However, the Speaker or presiding officer may allow more time. The House Rules also permit a reduction to as little as five minutes, at the Speaker's discretion (or that of chairman of the Committee of the Whole), when votes occur in sequence.

Voting on the House floor is almost always done in person. During the COVID-19 pandemic (2020–2022), however, Democratic leadership expanded the ability of members to cast votes by proxy. Under this system, a member could authorize a colleague to cast a vote on his or her behalf, with a statement to that effect read into the record. As the pandemic receded, proxy voting was criticized for becoming a tool for convenience, rather than public health. Members of both parties used the practice to attend other events instead of floor votes. Although Republican members took advantage of the proxy rules, their leadership sued (unsuccessfully) to ban the practice, and eventually repealed it once they reclaimed the majority in 2023.

The special rule reported by the Rules Committee may also stipulate how amendments are voted on to gain a parliamentary advantage. For example, a special rule may provide for a way to vote on several alternative amendments to the same language in the bill. Under the so-called "king of the hill" rule, several amendments are permitted, with the rule setting the order of consideration. Each amendment is voted on, and if more than one achieves a majority vote, the last one to be approved becomes the king of the hill, meaning that the bill is amended by that last successful amendment. Such provisions are sometimes referred to as "designer amendments."

An alternative inspired by the king of the hill procedure is the so-called "queen of the hill." Under this process, several alternative amendments to the same language are made in order, as in the king of the hill procedure. However, if more than one amendment receives a majority vote, the prevailing amendment is not the last one considered, but the one that received the most votes.

The special rule for consideration of a measure may also include a "self-executing rule." Under this procedure, a majority vote to adopt the special rule not only approves that rule but also "deems" the House to have passed a measure or adopted an amendment without a separate vote. Leadership often uses this tactic to avoid a separate vote on a matter that might be uncomfortable for some members of the majority caucus.

From 1979, until its repeal in 2011, the House had a standing rule known as the "Gephardt rule," which functioned in the same way. It provided for a self-executing House joint resolution to automatically lift the debt ceiling upon passage of the congressional budget resolution. This spared members from having to take a separate—and unpopular—vote to increase the statutory debt limit.

When the Committee of the Whole completes its work on a bill, the special rule typically provides that it automatically rises and reports the bill with a recommendation back to the House. The Speaker then returns to the chair and is handed the gavel from the chair of the Committee of the Whole.

J. Motion to Recommit

The minority party in the House has the right to offer a motion to recommit a matter to the committee of jurisdiction. These motions are frequently messaging votes, related only tangentially to the underlying bill and designed primarily to force the majority into an uncomfortable public vote. Although such motions are generally voted down by the majority, they allow the minority to secure a procedural vote framed to their advantage, compelling the majority to go on record on an issue they might prefer to avoid.

A motion to recommit may be made "with instructions," in which case ten minutes of debate are in order. If no instructions are included, the motion is non-debatable and a successful motion to recommit kills the bill.

K. Final Passage

Once the Committee of the Whole reports the bill back to the full House, the Speaker declares that, under the special rule, the previous question is ordered—the motion that ends debate and brings the matter to final votes. Thereafter, no further debate is in order, and no amendments not adopted in the Committee of the Whole may be offered. Separate votes on amendments adopted by the Committee of the Whole may occur if demanded by a member, unless prohibited under the special rule. On rare occasions, the House rejects controversial amendments adopted in the Committee of the Whole.

When all amendments have been disposed of, the measure is read for the third time (by title). After that reading, and before the vote on passage, a motion to recommit—usually offered by a member of the minority—is in order. Passage is determined by majority vote in the House. The bill is then reprinted as passed, marked with footer codes "EH" ("engrossed in the House") or "RS" ("received in the Senate").

Chapter 5
Senate Floor

A. Introduction

James Madison, before the U.S. Senate had even taken shape, recorded in his *Notes of Debates in the Federal Convention of 1787* that, on June 7, 1787, he rose to argue that "The use of the Senate is to consist in its proceeding with more coolness, with more system, and with more wisdom, than the popular branch."

Unlike the House of Representatives, the Senate was designed as a continuing body. Its rules have rarely changed since 1789 and, for the most part, have remained continuously in place. House rules, adopted and potentially changed every two years, favor the organized majority. By contrast, the Senate's rules and the precedents interpreting them have steadfastly protected the legislative minority and championed the independence of the individual senator.

These differences reflect the Founders' design for the Senate to stand as Madison's "necessary fence" against the dangers of overzealous majorities. In *The Federalist* No. 63, Madison wrote that "history informs us of no long-lived republic which had not a senate."

From the outset, the rules, precedents, and practices of the Senate were shaped to protect the privileges of the individual senator to debate and amend legislation and to guard against overzealous majorities. Even Thomas Jefferson, in a 1787 letter to James Madison, expressed concern:

> The instability of our laws is really a very serious inconvenience. I think that we ought to have obviated it by deciding that a whole year should always be allowed to elapse between the bringing in of a bill and the final passing of it. It should afterward be discussed and put to the vote without the possibility of making any alteration in it; and if the circumstances of the case required a more speedy decision, the question should not be decided by a simple majority, but by a majority of at least two-thirds of both houses.

The twin pillars of the Senate's unique rules are unlimited debate and unfettered amendments, principles that ensure that the minority can almost always exert some influence on legislative outcomes. This has often made the Senate the cradle of compromise. In the Senate, debate is largely unlimited and, in most circumstances, every senator has the right to offer non-germane amendments.

As former Majority Leader Robert Byrd (D-WV) once said, the Senate is "the last bastion of minority rights, where a minority can be heard, where a minority can stand on its feet, one individual if necessary, and speak until he falls into the dust."

Beneath the rules of the Senate is its bedrock Constitutional principle: equal representation of the states. Article I, Section 3 of the Constitution provides for two senators from each state, each casting one vote, and Article V qualifies the ability to amend the Constitution by guaranteeing that "no State, without its Consent, shall be deprived of its equal Suffrage in the Senate."

Originally, senators were elected by their respective state legislatures. Since 1913, when the Seventeenth Amendment to the Constitution was ratified, senators have been directly elected by the voters of their state.

The six-year term of office, the diversity of statewide constituencies, and the protections afforded by Senate rules and procedures lie at the root of each senator's fierce independence and formidable individual influence.

This chapter explores Senate floor procedures guided by those rules, precedents, and practices, including how legislation is scheduled, debated, amended and enacted. It sheds light on the complex maze of holds, filibusters, "amendment trees," and "legislative days."

B. Scheduling of Legislation

In the Senate, by precedent and tradition, the majority leader sets the agenda and decides which matters to call up for consideration on the floor. The majority leader's powers derive from the precedent that the position carries the privilege of prior recognition—meaning that if the majority leader seeks recognition, the presiding officer will always recognize them first.

Matters available for consideration appear on the Legislative Calendar (Senate Calendar of Business) or the Executive Calendar. The majority leader can bring a matter to the Senate floor in one of two ways: by moving to proceed to its consideration or by requesting unanimous consent to take it up. In most instances, the motion to proceed to a legislative matter is debatable and therefore subject to a filibuster.

Consideration of legislation on the Senate floor is generally more flexible than in the House. Although the Senate has formal standing rules and precedents that are often arcane and difficult to navigate, they are frequently set aside by unanimous consent. However, this flexibility can be counterbalanced by the potential for unlimited debate and numerous and sometimes non-germane amendments.

Individual senators, including those in the minority, wield considerable independent power, and their scheduling needs are often accommodated by the leadership. Because unanimous consent is frequently required in order to move forward expeditiously, and a single objection can prevent such an agreement, the majority leader is often forced to consult with the minority leader. This occurs on an ongoing basis, often at the floor-staff level. The leadership may negotiate any manner of scheduling and consideration.

These negotiations typically result in unanimous consent agreements, sometimes called "time agreements," worked out between the majority and minority leaders. Such agreements detail how the Senate will proceed and may involve lengthy discussions with numerous senators. Once reached, the agreement is formalized by the unanimous consent of the entire Senate— that is, when no objection is heard to the proposed terms. In other words, none of the hundred Senators verbally disapproves of an agreement; it is approved in the absence of an objection.

Unlike the House, all bills and resolutions in the Senate are placed on one calendar, called the "Calendar of General Orders," published daily in a pamphlet called the "Calendar of Business." The form of the measure (bill, joint resolution, concurrent resolution, or simple resolution) does not affect the order in which it might be called up.

C. Senate Calendars

There are two calendars maintained in the Senate and printed in separate pamphlets each day the Senate is in session. The "Calendar of Business," frequently referred to simply as "the Senate calendar," contains legislative matters, while the "Executive Calendar" lists treaties, nominations, and related measures.

Senate Rule VIII provides for a daily call of the "Calendar of Bills and Resolutions," understood to mean the section of the "Calendar of Business" labeled "Calendar of General Orders." Rule VII makes a call of that calendar mandatory on Mondays. These are among the many provisions of the Senate rules regarding routine procedures that are regularly circumvented by unanimous consent agreements put forward by the majority leader or their designee. This is done because following the arcane Senate rules precisely, particularly at the outset of every daily Senate session, is difficult and time consuming.

The Calendar of General Orders lists every bill and joint resolution reported by the Senate committees and any measures that were directly sent to the calendar by a senator pursuant to Rule XIV. Measures are listed in the order in which they were placed on the calendar.

The Executive Calendar lists all nominations and treaties available for floor action. Under Article II, Section 2 of the Constitution, the Senate has the power to confirm major presidential nominees—including all judicial nominees, many executive branch officials, and promotions of military officers—and to ratify treaties.

The Senate takes up measures listed on either calendar by unanimous consent or by a motion to proceed. Because unanimous consent requires the cooperation of all senators, a single senator can block the Senate from proceeding to the measure.

A motion to proceed to a measure may be made by any senator, though by Senate tradition the majority leader typically excercises this privilege. Legislation that has been on the calendar for one legislative day is eligible to be brought up by a simple majority vote on a motion to proceed. However, a motion to proceed is generally debatable in the Senate, meaning debate is unlimited. If such a motion is filibustered, Rule XXII requires a supermajority of 60 votes to invoke cloture and end debate.

Historically, filibusters on the motion to proceed were rare. Most senators treated the simple decision to take up a matter for debate and amendment as a routine step in the legislative process. As a consequence of increasing partisan polarization in the Senate, however, the minority party in recent Congresses has often sought to block motions to proceed to major legislative items they oppose, or simply to delay proceedings altogether, on the theory that all delay is good because it reduces the amount of legislation the majority party will be able to enact in any given session.

By precedent, a motion to proceed to a matter on the Executive Calendar (nominations or treaties) is not debatable. The majority leader decides whether to seek unanimous consent to proceed. In such cases, the leader or a designee makes the motion and waits for the presiding officer to declare that the Senate is in agreement if there are no objections. While a vote could occur, it is generally unnecessary.

D. Holds

When the majority leader intends to seek unanimous consent to take up a matter, advance notice is usually given to all senators. The principal way the majority leader's intent is communicated is by use of a "hotline," originally a telephone line connected to each office. Hotline messages are now sent via email through the party cloakrooms. Hotline messages are usually addressed immediately, giving senators the chance to object to the consideration of a matter—whether legislation, a nomination, or a treaty.

If a senator objects, this is communicated to the senator's party leadership staff. An objection implies that unanimous consent will not be granted, and that extended debate would likely occur if the majority leader were to move to proceed.

It is not uncommon for senators to object in response to hotline requests. The threatened objections are referred to as "holds." Holds are rooted in the traditions of senatorial courtesy and do not appear anywhere in the Senate rules. By tradition, the majority leader respects these holds. Senators are supposed to submit them in writing, but in practice they are often conveyed orally.

Some holds are made anonymously, and Senate leadership has traditionally honored requests for anonymity. In recent decades, however, efforts have been made to end the practice of these "secret holds." In 2007, senators were required to place a "notice of intent to object" in the *Congressional Record* within six days of Senate session. In 2011, that period was tightened to two days. These efforts have not been effective, as cooperation among two or more senators intent on holding a matter could extend the time indefinitely by rotating their holds, each lifting a hold before triggering the disclosure requirement while the other simultaneously places a new one.

Some holds simply request that leadership consult the senator before taking action on a measure.

A measure "clears" if no senator indicates their intention to object. In such cases, the majority leader will likely proceed with the proposed action. If the action is to "take up and pass" a bill or resolution by unanimous consent, the majority leader or designee will usually include it in a stack of measures and motions called up at the end of the day. This process is commonly referred to as "wrap-up." If the proposed action is to move to proceed to a matter on the calendar, the majority leader, once it has cleared, can schedule it with confidence that the motion to proceed will be agreed to by unanimous consent.

E. Unanimous Consent Agreements ("Time Agreements")

Most major pieces of legislation are considered in the Senate under unanimous consent agreements, frequently referred to as "time agreements." These agreements may limit general debate and debate on amendments, restrict the number of amendments to be considered, and, at times, specify a set time for the vote on final passage.

If a senator objects to a unanimous consent request to proceed to a measure, the majority leader may negotiate with all interested parties. However, if the leader concludes that overcoming objections would be too difficult or time-consuing, consideration of the measure may be postponed.

As an alternative, the majority leader may make a motion to proceed. This step is most often taken after unanimous consent to consider the matter has been blocked. A motion to proceed, however, is debatable in most circumstances, and therefore subject to unlimited debate. Ending debate to overcome a filibuster may require a cloture vote. Even if cloture is invoked, there can be up to 30 hours of consideration before a vote occurs on that motion to proceed. And this is simply to proceed to consider the legislation—not pass it. Only after the motion to proceed is adopted can the Senate begin to debate and amend the bill or resolution.

Negotiations to reach a time agreement on debate for a bill or resolution can be extensive and involve many senators. As a result, whether the decision is to use unanimous consent as the method to call up the legislation or risk a motion to proceed, individual senators have leverage to have their substantive concerns and scheduling needs considered. This gives senators far more procedural autonomy and influence than members of the House.

While Senate tradition and precedents put the majority leader in charge of the agenda, in practice the majority leader can rarely take up any controversial measure without consultation with and cooperation from the minority leader.

F. Consideration on the Senate Floor

When legislation reaches the Senate floor—whether by unanimous consent, a debatable motion to proceed, or a non-debatable motion to proceed under expedited procedures like those established by the 1974 Congressional Budget and Impoundment Control Act—the floor managers of the measure are usually the chair and ranking minority member of the committee that reported the legislation. The adoption of a bill or resolution by the Senate often requires the relevant committee chair, as the principal floor manager, to work closely and cooperatively with the ranking minority member of the committee. Of course, there are occasions when this relationship is strained. For example, there are times when the majority has the votes necessary to enact the measure without minority input and thus might not be in a compromising mood.

Floor debate customarily begins with opening statements by the floor managers. Under Senate Rules VII, VIII, XV, XVI, XXII, however, the legislation is subject to amendment as soon as it is called up. If the measure is considered under a unanimous consent agreement or pursuant to expedited procedures, amendments may be controlled and limited by the provisions of the agreement or the law.

G. Quorum Calls

A common feature of debate on the Senate floor is the quorum call, some of which last for hours. The roll is called at a very slow pace. The slow pace is to prevent completing the entire roll without a quorum having presented itself. Under the rules (Senate Rules XII, XX, and XXII), should a quorum call reveal the lack of a quorum, the Senate would then be required either to produce a quorum, or to adjourn. These slow-motion quorum calls are a way for the Senate leadership to conduct negotiations with other senators. Such negotiations can be complex and protracted. If successful, the outcome is often a unanimous consent agreement breaking a deadlock.

When a quorum call becomes a serious effort to bring enough senators to the Senate floor to establish a quorum, it is known as a "live quorum." Senators are notified that a vote is in progress to produce a quorum, and they usually proceed to the Senate floor to be recorded on that vote. Article I, Section 5 of the Constitution provides that each body can "compel the Attendance of absent Members...." In 1798, the Senate adopted a rule enforcing senators' attendance. When the majority leader seeks to ensure a quorum, Senate Rule VI provides that "a majority of the Senators present may direct the Sergeant at Arms to request, and, when necessary, to compel the attendance of the absent Senators." A motion to instruct the sergeant-at-arms to compel the attendance of absent senators is made and a vote is held, the purpose of which is to produce a quorum, making the motion to compel moot.

One dramatic example occurred in 1988 during an all-night filibuster of a campaign finance reform bill. With the Republican minority attempting to deny him a quorum, Majority Leader Robert Byrd made a motion to instruct the Senate sergeant-at-arms to arrest absent senators in order to bring them to the chamber. The Senate voted 45-3 to authorize the arrests. Article 1, Section 5 of the Constitution provides that "a smaller Number ... [than the default quorum of a majority of senators] may be authorized to compel the Attendance of absent Members." Senator Bob Packwood (R-OR) was carried into the Senate chamber to help establish the quorum. The Senate sergeant-at-arms had located Sen. Packwood hiding out in his office, had the door removed from its hinges, and hauled him into the chamber.

H. Filibuster

The Constitution provides each chamber the authority to establish and revise its own rules. Article I, Section 5, Clause 2 states, "Each House may determine the Rules of its Proceedings." In the Senate, the most prominent feature produced by the rules of its proceedings has come to be called the filibuster.

Senate Rule XIX states that "the Presiding Officer shall recognize the Senator who shall first address him" and that "no Senator shall interrupt another

Senator in debate without his consent." This rule, combined with the absence in the Senate rules of a "previous question motion," i.e., a motion to end debate and vote on the matter before the body, assures that each senator has the privilege of unlimited debate and that the minority has leverage.

Debate in the Senate can only be constrained in four ways: by invoking cloture; by unanimous consent; by adopting a motion to table (which defeats the question); or by operating under expedited procedures established in laws such as the 1974 Budget Act. Rule XIX also states that "no Senator shall speak more than twice upon any one question in debate on the same legislative day without leave of the Senate." This so-called "two-speech rule" has not proven an effective way to break a filibuster because "any one question" has been interpreted in such a way that a senator who makes a motion or offers an amendment is then able to make two speeches on those matters.

As a result, a senator or group of senators may delay action on an amendment or the legislation itself, or block them entirely. Any matter subject to unlimited debate under the Senate rules may be filibustered.

During debate, if a senator simply yields to another senator, the chair may rule that the floor has been relinquished. However, a senator may yield to another colleague for a question and still retain control of the floor. In practice, this is sometimes used to assist a senator intent on holding the floor for an extended period. The colleague will ask, "Will the senator yield for a question?"—often adding, "without losing your right to the floor" for clarity. What follows are often long, meandering questions designed to use time and relieve the filibustering senator.

Since the rules do not provide a means—aside from cloture—to force a vote, the filibuster can be effective even with no one holding the floor. This can make reaching a vote on an amendment (except to table it, which defeats it) or on final passage potentially extremely difficult or even impossible.

Cloture, under Senate Rule XXII, requires a vote of three-fifths of senators duly chosen and sworn—60 votes when the Senate has its full 100 members— to end debate. The process to "invoke cloture" originates with a "cloture motion" signed by at least sixteen senators. The cloture vote automatically occurs, under Senate Rule XXII, one hour after the Senate has convened on the second calendar day on which the Senate is in session after the cloture motion is made. A quorum call precedes the vote on cloture, though it is often dispensed with by unanimous consent, and the Senate may also agree by unanimous consent to hold the vote at a more convenient time.

Even when cloture is invoked, Rule XXII provides an additional 30 hours of consideration, which includes time consumed in debate, quorum calls, and roll call votes. In the polarized atmosphere of recent years, those on the losing side of a cloture vote have insisted on using the full 30 hours, mostly for delay and obstruction.

Amendments offered after cloture is invoked must be germane. At times, this may be the majority leader's main objective in securing early cloture on a measure.

Because all senators know that any amendment or legislation proposed in the Senate may require that supermajority of 60 votes, they usually begin immediately searching for a cosponsor for their proposal from the other side of the aisle. This fosters negotiation, compromise, and moderation—in other words, legislating.

Critics of the filibuster argue that its expanded use in recent years has turned it largely into a tool of obstruction, shifting control of the Senate from the majority to the minority party. For much of its history the filibuster endured because senators excercised restraint, understanding that overuse could invite efforts to abolish it. But in recent decades its use has surged, alongside other procedural maneuvers: filling the amendment tree, invoking Senate Rule XIV to circumvent committees, relying on the reconciliation process under the Budget Act, employing the "nuclear option" to distort the interpretation of Senate rules, and making greater use of holds.

It is difficult to count filibusters, because it is not always clear that a filibuster is occurring. Usually it is the cloture votes that are counted, but they can occur when there is no filibuster. The majority leader may use a cloture vote to preclude the possibility of a filibuster or to exclude non-germane amendments. Also, the existence of a filibuster needn't always lead to a cloture vote. Sometimes a compromise is reached or one side gives up. Nonetheless, the best approximation of the increase in filibusters is to look at the increase in cloture votes.

The cloture rule was adopted by the Senate in 1917. Prior to that time, from 1806 when the previous question motion was dropped, there was no way to end debate until all senators were ready to vote. Even before 1806, the previous question motion was not used to cut off debate. From 1917 through 1970, a total of only 49 cloture votes were held. Beginning in 1971, this began to change. In the 92nd and 93rd Congresses (1971–1974), 51 cloture votes were held. Beginning in 1991, no single Congress (two-year period) has seen fewer than 46 cloture votes.

Defenders of the filibuster argue that the solution to excessive partisanship and the deterioration of Senate comity is not to rewrite Senate rules. They say that eliminating the filibuster, in fact, would deepen polarization, and they emphasize its role as both a safeguard for minority rights and a force for consensus-building.

There are two exceptions to the 60-vote requirement in the Senate's rules and precedents regarding cloture. First, when the Senate is considering a change to its Standing Rules, cloture can only be invoked by a two-thirds vote, a quorum being present. This requirement makes changes in the Senate rules extremely difficult to accomplish because ending debate requires 67 votes if all senators are voting.

Second, cloture ending debate on the confirmation of executive branch or judicial nominations requires only a simple majority vote, under precedents established in 2013 by Senate Democrats and in 2017 by Senate Republicans using the "nuclear option." The simple majority threshold is frequently misunderstood to mean 51 affirmative votes (or 50 votes plus the deciding vote of the vice president). As the Senate Parliamentarian has interpreted the 2013 and 2017 precedents, cloture could be invoked by a plurality of the Senate, provided a quorum is present. In theory, this could be as few as 26 votes required to invoke cloture on confirmation of a nomination.

I. The Nuclear Option

In November 2013, Majority Leader Harry Reid (D-NV) executed a parliamentary maneuver labeled the "nuclear option." This was accomplished by raising a point of order that "the votes on cloture under Rule XXII for all nominations other than for the Supreme Court of the United States is by majority vote." The President *pro tempore* of the Senate, Senator Patrick Leahy (D-VT), acting on the advice of the parliamentarian, ruled, "Under the rules, the point of order is not sustained." The Democratic majority then overturned the Leahy ruling on a non-debatable motion to appeal. Senator Leahy himself voted to overturn his own ruling. In this way, Senate Democrats created a precedent that the Senate Rule XXII provision stating that ending debate requires a vote of "three-fifths of the Senators duly chosen and sworn" would now be interpreted to mean a simple majority, except for nominations to the Supreme Court, which would still require a 60-vote supermajority. In 2017, Senate Republicans extended the precedent to Supreme Court nominations, reducing the threshold there to a simple majority as well.

Beyond the impact of the nuclear option on the nomination process, those who defend the filibuster are concerned that the precedent could be used again in the future to eliminate the filibuster for legislative matters. In 2010, just a few months before his death, Senator Robert Byrd wrote:

> If the rules are abused, and Senators exhaust the patience of their colleagues, such actions can invite draconian measures. But those measures themselves can, in the long run, be as detrimental to the role of the institution and to the rights of the American people as the abuse of the rules.

Senator Kyrsten Sinema (I-AZ) occupied one of the Senate's key swing votes in the early 2020s, alongside Senator Joe Manchin (D-WV). She occasionally referred to her decision to defend the filibuster, against significant pressure from Democrats, as one of the most important votes of her career.

For more than 200 years, since the removal of the previous question motion from the Standing Rules, the Senate has defended the privilege accorded to individual senators to speak without limit. In April 2017, a bipartisan group of 61 senators sent a letter to the Senate's leadership expressing opposition to "...any effort to curtail the existing rights and prerogatives of Senators to engage in full, robust, and extended debate..." Nearly seven decades earlier, in March 1949, then-Senator Lyndon Johnson declared:

> If I should have the opportunity to send into the countries behind the iron curtain one freedom and only one, I know what my choice would be. I would send to those nations the right of unlimited debate in their legislative chambers. Peter the Great did not have a Senate with unlimited debate, with power over the purse, when he enslaved hundreds of thousands of men in the building of Saint Petersburg. If we now, in haste and irritation, shut off this freedom, we shall be cutting off the most vital safeguard which minorities possess against the tyranny of momentary majorities.

As other norms and precedents erode, the Senate's institutional defenders continue to emphasize the importance of this key feature of the upper chamber.

J. Amendment on the Senate Floor and In Committee

A bill or resolution that reaches the Senate floor is normally subject to amendment by both individual senators and by the committee that reported it.

Committee amendments take priority. When a committee amendment is pending, it is subject to further amendment, but no other amendments are in order except to the language addressed by that committee amendment.

If the committee reported a total substitute for the text of the measure, the substitute is voted on last since its adoption would preclude further amendment. This is because amendments are not in order to portions of a measure already amended, unless the new amendment takes a "bigger bite"—that is, it addresses the already-amended portion in the course of changing a broader portion of text.

Committee amendments are often adopted by unanimous consent. Consent may also be given to consider the committee amendments as original text. This means that further amendment to parts of the measure—or to the entire measure if a total substitute was adopted—would be considered in the first degree.

The number of amendments allowed, whether they must be germane, and even which specific amendments are in order can be set by a unanimous consent agreement governing debate and amendment on a particular measure. Absent unanimous consent or cloture, debate on amendments is not limited, and amendments need not be germane (strictly related by subject matter) to the bill. Non-germane amendments are often called "riders."

There are exceptions under Senate rules (Senate Rules XVI and XXII) and the Congressional Budget and Impoundment Act (Section 305(b)), which requires germaneness for appropriations bills, measures under the Budget Act, and amendments offered after cloture has been invoked. A unanimous consent agreement may also impose a germaneness requirement. When germaneness is required in the Senate, precedents impose a stricter standard than in the House.

Amendments are either in the "first degree," meaning they change the text of the measure before the Senate, or in the "second degree," meaning they amend a first-degree amendment. No third-degree amendments are in order.

A "perfecting amendment," if adopted, changes the text of the measure to which it is offered. "Substitute amendments" replace all available text with new language.

After adoption of an amendment, a senator invariably moves to "reconsider the vote." This motion to reconsider is normally routinely made by a senator from the prevailing side or one who did not vote and immediately tabled, thus killing the possibility of a revote on the matter. If the motion to reconsider were adopted, the Senate would vote again on the original matter.

In the Senate, different amendment trees are possible based on the form of the initial amendment offered. One tree is designed for motions to strike and insert, another for a motion to insert, a third for a motion to strike, and a fourth for a motion to strike all the text of a measure and insert completely new text, which is a complete substitute for a measure.

K. Filling the Amendment Tree

The Senate amendment tree is considerably more complex than in the House. Under the most complex scenario—which only occurs under limited circumstances and if all of the amendments are offered in a particular order—there could be as many as 11 amendments pending at the same time. Such highly complex trees are rare. Amendments are added to the tree in the order they are offered and are voted upon in the reverse order of their submission.

In recent years, the majority leader has more frequently used the tactic of purposely filling the amendment tree. Like the House version, the Senate amendment tree is a diagram showing the types and number of amendments permitted to be simultaneously pending in the Senate at a given time and under a given parliamentary situation. Four charts in *Riddick's Senate Procedure* (most recently prepared and edited in 1992 by former Senate parliamentarians Floyd Riddick and Alan Frumin, S. Doc. 101-28) depict possible Senate amendment trees and are reproduced on the following pages.

Senate Amendment to Insert

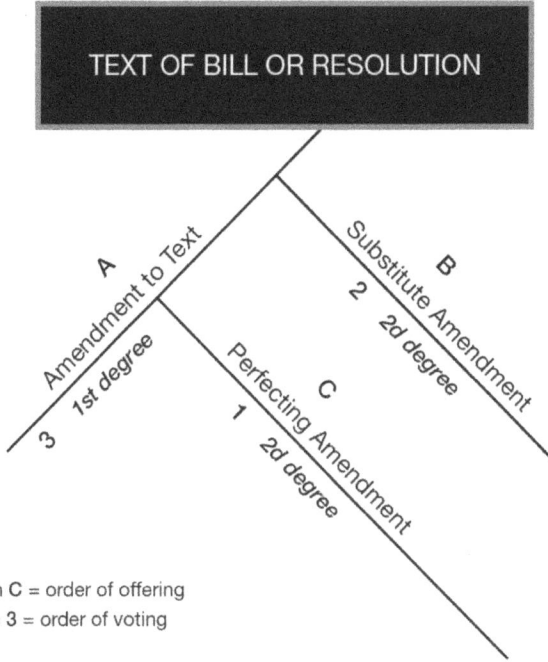

TEXT OF BILL OR RESOLUTION

A — Amendment to Text — 1st degree — 3

B — Substitute Amendment — 2d degree — 2

C — Perfecting Amendment — 2d degree — 1

A through C = order of offering
1 through 3 = order of voting

Senate Amendment to Strike

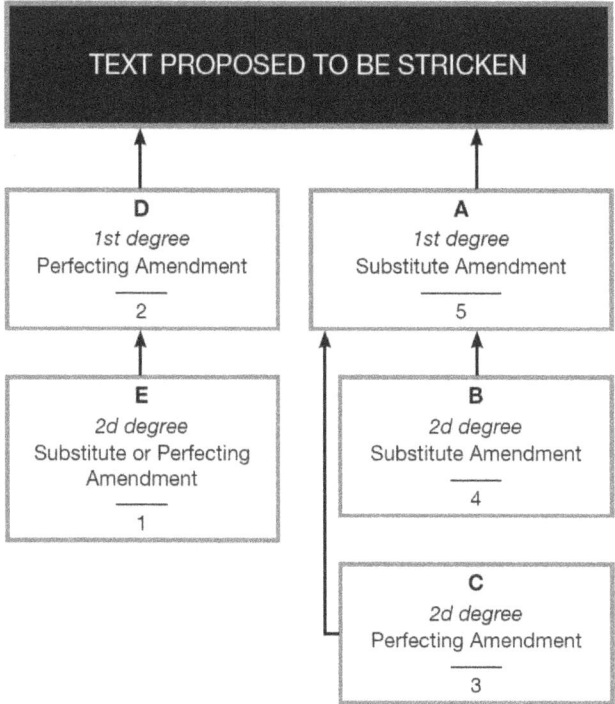

TEXT PROPOSED TO BE STRICKEN

D	A
1st degree	*1st degree*
Perfecting Amendment	Substitute Amendment
——	——
2	5

E	B
2d degree	*2d degree*
Substitute or Perfecting	Substitute Amendment
Amendment	——
——	4
1	

C
2d degree
Perfecting Amendment
——
3

A through **E** = order of offering to get all of the above
amendments before the Senate

1 through **5** = order of voting

Senate Amendment to Strike and Insert
(Substitute for Section of a Bill)

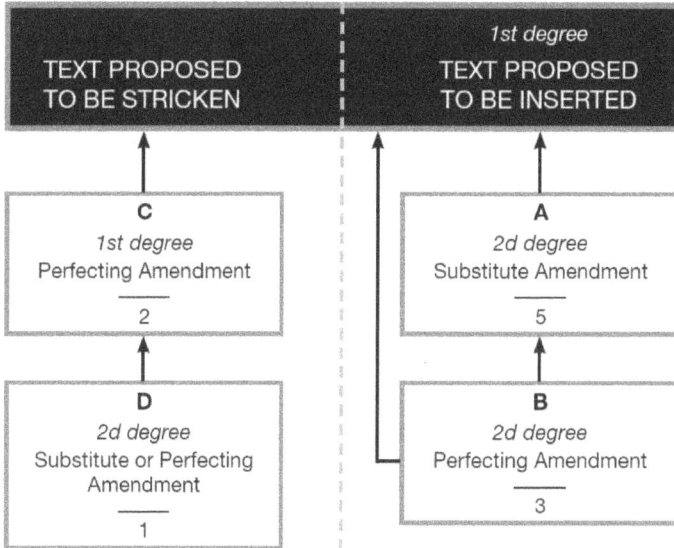

TEXT PROPOSED TO BE STRICKEN	*1st degree* TEXT PROPOSED TO BE INSERTED

C
1st degree
Perfecting Amendment
———
2

A
2d degree
Substitute Amendment
———
5

D
2d degree
Substitute or Perfecting Amendment
———
1

B
2d degree
Perfecting Amendment
———
3

A through **D** = order of offering to get all of the above amendments before the Senate

1 through **4** = order of voting

Senate Amendment to Strike and Insert
(Substitute for Bill)

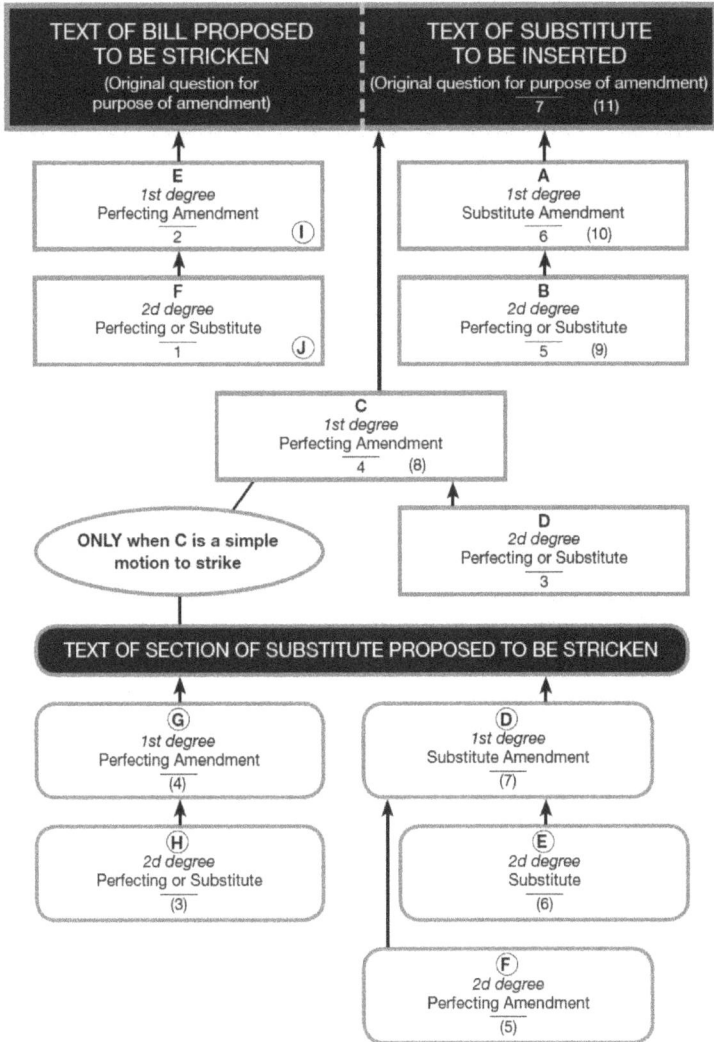

TEXT OF BILL PROPOSED TO BE STRICKEN	TEXT OF SUBSTITUTE TO BE INSERTED
(Original question for purpose of amendment)	(Original question for purpose of amendment) $\frac{}{7}$ (11)

E
1st degree
Perfecting Amendment
$\frac{}{2}$ (I)

A
1st degree
Substitute Amendment
$\frac{}{6}$ (10)

F
2d degree
Perfecting or Substitute
$\frac{}{1}$ (J)

B
2d degree
Perfecting or Substitute
$\frac{}{5}$ (9)

C
1st degree
Perfecting Amendment
$\frac{}{4}$ (8)

ONLY when **C** is a simple motion to strike

D
2d degree
Perfecting or Substitute
$\frac{}{3}$

TEXT OF SECTION OF SUBSTITUTE PROPOSED TO BE STRICKEN

(G)
1st degree
Perfecting Amendment
$\frac{}{(4)}$

(D)
1st degree
Substitute Amendment
$\frac{}{(7)}$

(H)
2d degree
Perfecting or Substitute
$\frac{}{(3)}$

(E)
2d degree
Substitute
$\frac{}{(6)}$

(F)
2d degree
Perfecting Amendment
$\frac{}{(5)}$

A through **J** = order of offering to have all amendments pending at the same time
1 through **11** = order of voting
Circled and parenthetical material apply only when **C** is a motion to strike

As in the House, even if otherwise in order, amendments may be constrained by the absence of room on the amendment tree. The tree indicates the order that amendments, if offered, are voted on.

"Filling the amendment tree" describes purposely offering a sufficient series of amendments one after the other to occupy each branch of the tree. Once this occurs, no further amendments are in order unless and until an amendment is disposed of by the Senate. The amendments occupying the tree may be disposed of if the Senate votes to adopt or defeat the amendment or the amendment is tabled, killing it. Amendments can also be withdrawn or removed by a point of order sustained by the presiding officer.

In theory, any member of the Senate could fill the tree by offering a series of amendments designed to occupy all of the branches. As a practical matter, only the majority leader can be assured of holding the floor to offer the sufficient number of amendments to fill the tree, due to their "right of prior recognition." Once a senator offers an amendment, they lose the floor; only the majority leader can be certain of being recognized again immediately by the presiding officer to offer another amendment.

When wielded by the majority leader, filling the tree can be a powerful tool to constrain the minority's ability to offer amendments. A majority leader can fill the tree as a way of completely controlling the flow and timing of amendments, allowing only those they approve. By asking unanimous consent to temporarily set aside the amendment on the outermost branch of the tree, the majority leader may permit approved amendments to be considered. In this way the majority leader becomes the gatekeeper.

When filling the tree is combined with the filing of a cloture motion, the leader can attempt to both cut off debate and limit amendments on the measure.

The ability to offer amendments is one of the pillars of minority rights in the Senate. Filling the tree discourages debate, compromise, and bipartisan negotiation. It frustrates the minority, whose members might in response launch a filibuster on the measure and cease cooperation, leading to gridlock on the floor.

At times, the minority acts first in response to the suspicion that the majority will file cloture at the very beginning of deliberation on the legislation. In such circumstances, the minority have on occasion filibustered the motion to proceed to the bill, holding it hostage, and then demanded the right to offer their amendments when the bill is taken up. It can be difficult for observers and participants to know where the resultant gridlock began. Often both sides feel aggrieved by the tactics being used by the opposing party.

Historically, filling the amendment tree was used sparingly and usually as a way to temporarily block amendments to encourage or force the minority leader to negotiate with the majority leader on a time agreement to limit amendments to the measure.

In 2013, the Senate adopted a standing order which has the force of a Senate rule—effective for the 113th Congress only—that sought to protect the minority's ability to offer at least two amendments at the beginning of consideration of a measure. In the face of continued battles over Senate procedures, the standing order was not renewed in succeeding Congresses.

L. Calendar Days and Legislative Days

Several Senate rules set days when an action may occur. Some specify "calendar days." For example, Senate Rule XIII governing motions to reconsider reads, "When a question has been decided by the Senate, any senator voting with the prevailing side or who has not voted may, on *the same day or on either of the next two days of actual session* thereafter, move a reconsideration..." (emphasis added). By precedent, the Senate interprets that language to mean a calendar day, which is a normal twenty-four-hour period.

Other rules refer to, or have been construed to mean, a "legislative day" or "session day." For example, Senate Rule VIII, which details the "order of business," states: "All motions made during the first two hours of a *new legislative day* to proceed to the consideration of any matter shall be determined without debate..." (emphasis added). A legislative day starts when the Senate convenes after an adjournment and continues until the Senate next adjourns. This means that a legislative day can last for a number of calendar days or even weeks or months if the Senate ends one or more successive daily sessions by recessing rather than adjourning.

Because the Senate rules (IV, VII, VIII) provide for a number of burdensome procedures at the outset of each legislative day, the majority leader frequently, before adjournment, requests unanimous consent to dispense with those procedures for the next legislative day. Without that consent, the majority leader may seek to "recess" the Senate rather than adjourning, thereby continuing the same legislative day. For example, Majority Leader Robert Byrd kept the Senate in one very long legislative day from January 3 to June 12 in 1980.

Counting legislative days becomes crucial in election years when party control of Congress and the presidency both change. Under the Congressional Review Act, Congress can overturn major rules by passing a joint resolution of disapproval for the new president's signature. The major rules subject to this negative power are those submitted to Congress within a "lookback period" of 60 legislative or session days.

M. Voting

The Senate conducts votes by three methods: roll call (often referred to as "the yeas and nays"), voice, and division (Senate Rule XII).

Any senator may request the yeas and nays. If the request is seconded by at least one-fifth of a quorum—no fewer than eleven senators—the presiding officer will state that "the yeas and nays are ordered." When the debate on the matter is concluded, the clerk calls the roll. A roll call vote is generally limited to fifteen minutes, with a customary five-minute grace period; however, the majority leader may hold the vote open longer to accommodate senators having difficulty getting to the floor on time. When many votes are scheduled in a "stack," the period for voting is often reduced by unanimous consent to ten minutes. An example is the often extensive list of consecutive roll call votes, known as a "vote-a-rama," which occurs at the end of debate on a budget resolution or reconciliation bill.

A voice vote occurs when no roll call is demanded. Often when unanimous consent is sought, the presiding officer declares, "without objection (the matter) is agreed to." If the voice vote is actually carried out, the presiding office will ask for those in favor to say "aye" and those opposed "nay." The presiding officer will announce the judgment based on the loudness of each side's vote, stating tentatively, e.g., "the ayes appear to have it… the ayes do have it and the [question] is agreed to." At the point indicated by the ellipses, a senator may ask for a recorded vote if not satisfied that the presiding officer has judged correctly. This seldom occurs.

Finally, on rare occasions, a division or "standing vote" will be demanded by a senator or requested by the presiding officer. Senators on each side of the question are asked to stand and be counted. On a division vote, no record is made of how individual senators voted.

N. Final Passage

When all amendments have been disposed of, the measure is "engrossed" and "read for the third time" (by title). (Senate Rule XIV).

Following the vote on passage, as with an amendment or motion, a senator on the prevailing side makes a motion to reconsider (Rules XIII, XV, XXII) and normally this is immediately tabled by voice vote. Occasionally a cloture vote to end debate and move to the vote on final passage is close, but does not succeed. The majority leader, to preserve the ability to try again on cloture at a later time, will "enter" a motion to reconsider. The motion is placed on a special calendar and may be brought up at a future time by unanimous consent or a motion to proceed to it. In an action that often confuses many observers of the Senate, the majority leader at the end of a cloture vote that narrowly failed will change his/her vote from in favor of cloture to against. Because a senator must be on the prevailing side in order to be eligible to enter the motion to reconsider, the majority leader will switch sides.

Once a measure has been passed by the Senate, the enrollment clerk sends the measure to the Government Publishing Office to be officially printed. Certified by the Secretary of the Senate, this is called the "engrossed bill" or an "engrossed Senate amendmen" to a House-originated bill.

Engrossed bills and amendments are "messaged" to the House of Representatives.

If the measure passed by the Senate was a measure previously passed by the House and the text remained identical to the House passed measure, it is "enrolled (printed on parchment paper)," signed by the Speaker and the president of the Senate (sometimes the President *pro tempore* or another senator authorized by the Senate), and sent to the president.

Chapter 6
Resolving Differences Between the House and Senate

Table of Sections

A. Introduction

For any legislation to become law, under the Constitution, Article 1, Section 7, both the House and the Senate most pass the *same* measure. Only when the text of the bill or joint resolution is identical in both chambers is it sent to the president.

Legislating in Congress involves negotiation, compromise, moderation, and civility. The process of resolving differences between the chambers is no different. While the Congress of recent decades has made legislative compromise seemingly unreachable at times, the Constitution and the rules of the House and Senate compel the chambers to reach accommodation, at least in some circumstances.

This process is often very difficult and complex. Even when the House and Senate share the same majority party, and the president is also of that party, it still may not be simple. Differing policy views and politics between the chambers or with the president can derail the effort.

But when the chambers are run by different parties, it is even more challenging, sometimes insurmountable.

B. Resolving Differences

One chamber must ultimately pass the product of the other, or they must agree on language added or subtracted. Either way, in the end, the Senate must consider a House measure or the House must consider a Senate measure.

When the first chamber to act passes a measure, it sends ("messages") an engrossed copy of the legislation to the other body. In the second chamber, the measure may be "held at the desk" or referred to the appropriate committee.

The easiest case is if the House passes without amendment legislation sent to it by the Senate, simply adopting the Senate measure, or vice versa. This process usually occurs on measures that are not controversial. When the same party controls both chambers, the House and Senate leadership may take this as the course of least resistance. For example, the passage of the Affordable Care Act, one of the most controversial bills of recent decades, was ultimately passed in this fashion. The Democrats at the time controlled both the House and the Senate. The substance of the bill was first passed by the Senate at 7:00 a.m. on Christmas morning in 2009, by a 60-39 party-line vote, inserted into the text of a minor, unrelated House-passed bill. The House passed without amendment the Senate-amended House bill on March 21 of the following year and sent it to President Barack Obama, who signed the bill into law on March 23.

Even with control of both chambers—and a 60-vote filibuster-proof majority in the Senate—the Democratic leadership knew that the minority in the Senate could use a conference committee or amendments between the houses to make passage extremely difficult. They therefore opted for House acceptance of the Senate bill.

If the chamber receiving the legislation does not pass identical language, it may amend the measure—sometimes replacing it entirely. For example, if the House sends the Senate a bill on a matter the Senate has been working on seperately, the Senate will hold the House bill at the desk and vote to amend it with its own version.

If differences between the House and Senate legislation cannot be resolved by "amendments between the houses," they may convene a conference committee, a temporary committee made up of House and Senate members and staffed by the professional staff of the committee with jurisdiction over the bills. If the conference committee is able to reach agreement on language acceptable to the conferees from each chamber, the committee issues a conference report, which must be passed without amendment by each chamber before going to the president's desk. In this case, the "conference report" is actual legislative text, not merely expository or directive report language like that issued by a committee. The conference report text is accompanied by a "joint explanatory statement" or "statement of managers," which serves many of the same functions as standard committee report language.

C. Amendments Between the Chambers

When a measure is messaged from one chamber to the other and the second chamber amends it, the legislation is returned to the body that originally passed it.

The originating chamber then may accept the amendment. In this case, both houses having passed the bill or resolution in identical form, it is sent to the president.

In the House, the floor manager of the legislation might ask the House to "concur" in the Senate amendment. In the Senate, the manager may request unanimous consent to concur in the House amendment. In either case, if approved, the bill or resolution is sent to the president's desk.

However, the originating chamber has the opportunity to further amend the legislation and send it back to the other chamber. For example, the House might concur in a Senate amendment with a further amendment. If this is agreed to, normally by unanimous consent, the House-passed measure with the "House amendment to the Senate amendment to the House bill" is returned to the Senate.

In much the same way, the Senate can concur in a House amendment with a further Senate amendment. However, in the Senate, although the motion to proceed to the House amendment to the Senate measure is non-debatable, the actual consideration of the House amendment to which the Senate has concurred or concurred with a further amendment is debatable and could be subject to filibuster. Therefore, if unanimous consent cannot be obtained (it usually is at this point), the chambers may need to consider a conference committee.

This back-and-forth exchange of amendments can occur multiple times. Colloquially, this back and forth series of amendments is known as "ping ponging" the bill. It can add significant delay and uncertainty, and is a disfavored course of action for "must-pass" legislation.

If at some point in the process either body decides not to act on the legislation sent to it by the other chamber, the leadership may decide to seek a conference with the other chamber. Otherwise, if neither chamber is willing to relent, the legislation may die. Going to conference is a three-step process in either chamber.

D. Conference

A conference committee is a temporary, ad hoc committee of House members and senators formed to draft a compromise bill that both chambers can accept. A conference cannot be held unless and until both chambers formally agree to participate.

Convening a conference requires three steps in each chamber.

The first step is to formally disagree with the version sent to it by the other chamber and insist on its own measure. Usually, the chamber that first approved the measure acts first, but the second chamber may "insist on its amendments" and then request a conference.

Step two is to request a conference.

The final step toward convening a conference committee is the appointment of conferees by the presiding officer. The conference is formed only if the second chamber insists on its amendment, accepts the request for a conference, and appoints its conferees.

In the Senate, each of these three steps is carried out by debatable motion. Since debatable matters in the Senate are generally subject to filibuster, there can sometimes be a problem getting the measure to conference if a significant number of senators (41 to oppose cloture) are sufficiently opposed to the legislation that they do not want a conference committee to be convened.

Until 2013, a determined group of senators—or even a single senator—could create an enormous obstacle to the formation of a conference committee by filibustering each of the three required motions. This made the process time-consuming and potentially insurmountable.

That year, the Senate amended its standing rules to allow the three necessary motions to be combined into a single, non-divisible motion, reducing the number of possible filibusters from three to one. The same rules change also cut the post-cloture debate time on this motion from 30 hours to two. Senate Rule XXVIII reflects these changes.

When a conference is convened, each chamber names conferees. In the House, the Speaker appoints conferees. In the Senate, the presiding officer—typically empowered by unanimous consent—names the conferees, formally known as "managers on the part of the Senate." These decisions in both bodies are generally made through consultation with the committee chair and the party leadership. Usually senior members of the committees of jurisdiction are appointed, but there is wide discretion. Conferees may include junior members, members who do not sit on the committee of jurisdiction, or members of the leadership team.

The number of conferees from each chamber can range widely. Since conference committee decisions are made by the majority of each delegation as opposed to a majority vote of all conferees, the relative size of House and Senate delegations plays no significant role, and each chamber may name as many conferees as it chooses.

In the House, a motion to instruct conferees may be offered. If adopted, it expresses the chamber's preference but is not binding. Such motions are rare in the Senate, where they are debatable, subject to amendment, and potentially subject to a filibuster.

While conference committees have wide latitude as to how they conduct their negotiations, they are limited in "scope" by the rules of both chambers. That is, they may not consider language not passed by either chamber, nor add new spending provisions—whether specific discretionary appropriations or mandatory spending—not contained in either the House- or Senate-passed bill. Novel material added in conference is sometimes described as "airdropped" into the conference report. In recent years, an airdrop has generally required the unanimous agreement of chamber leadership, and support from at least the majority in each committee with jurisdiction.

If House members believe a conference has exceeded its authority by including provisions outside its scope, a point of order may be raised. Such challenges are rare, and to preclude them the House Rules Committee may adopt a special rule for the conference report that waives all points of order.

In the Senate, Rule XXVIII also allows a point of order if the conference report exceeds the scope of the conference. It can be waived by a three-fifths vote of senators chosen and sworn (usually sixty). In 1996, the Senate overruled such a point of order, effectively negating the rule by precedent. No "out of scope" rule applied until the Senate reinstated the application of the rule at the start of the 107th Congress five years later.

Some conferences are more formal than others. Actual formal meetings of the conference committees can be as few as one (known as "passing the gavel"). In some cases informal closed meetings, particularly of the majority members, can resolve the differences and present the conference with a fait accompli. Few formal rules govern conference procedures, and committees that frequently pass legislation rely on multiple sets of internal procedures to organize and streamline the process. Professional staff and senior members of those committees often meet repeatedly to negotiate text, elevate deadlocked issues, and sound out members on positions likely to affect final passage.

In recent Congresses, formal conferences have become less common. Political polarization has led to more powerful central leadership in both chambers and those leaders are more likely to want to keep control of the process of resolving differences and negotiating bicameral agreements. Particularly when both chambers are controlled by the same party, the House and Senate leadership may seek to avoid a full-scale conference to reduce minority party involvement in the decisions and minimize opportunities for obstruction.

E. Conference Reports

When a conference committee completes its work, it will recommend that either the House recede from all or certain of its amendments, the Senate recede from all or certain of its amendments, or both. Rarely will a conference committee report the inability to reach an agreement. A majority of each chamber's delegations to the conference is necessary to approve a report for submission to the House and Senate.

Informal "pre-conferences" allow committee staff to work out differences in advance, as a way of facilitating the work of the formal conference if one is held. On occasion, pre-conferencing begins even before the second chamber has completed action on the bill. During conference, advocates, non-conferees, and other members have an opportunity to relitigate provisions that were included in either chamber's version of the bill. Conferees decide whether to adopt or drop provisions that appear in just one of the bills, and how to resolve textual differences between similar provisions. Professional staff submit negotiated outcomes to legislative counsel offices, who assist in drafting the final conference language.

When one chamber accepts the other's position, it is said to "recede" to the second. For instance, if the House-passed version of a bill contained a provision that had no analogue in the Senate, and the conference agrees to adopt the House provision, the provision is included and a joint explanatory statement notes that "the Senate recedes." A chamber may recede "with amendment," meaning that a provision is included but with textual adjustments negotiated in conference.

If a chamber agrees to drop its own provision that has no counterpart in the other bill, that sponsoring chamber recedes and the provision is omitted from the conference report. The joint explanatory statement collects such outcomes in sections captioned: "Legislative Provisions Not Adopted," shorthanded to "LPNA." That outcome does not necessarily end an issue. In discussing an LPNA outcome, joint explanatory statement language can direct an official to take action consistent with the dropped provision, typically to provide a report or a briefing to the committees. Practitioners are thus well advised to read the entire JES carefully, including those sections that discuss legislative provisions that were not adopted in formal bill text.

When provisions in both bills are true "mirror images," without even stylistic differences between them, they are usually deemed agreed. Those provisions are closed to further amendments in conference.

Once the conference committee has reached agreement, conferees must indicate their approval by signing both the conference report and the joint statement. The conference report is not open to further amendment. In the first chamber to consider the conference, a member can move to recommit the bill to the conference committee. But once the first chamber has passed the conference report, the conference committee is dissolved and the second chamber to act can no longer recommit the bill to the conference because it no longer exists.

In both the Senate and the House, a conference report is a privileged matter. In the House this means that once the official papers are received the conference report can be taken up at almost any time. In the Senate this means that the motion to proceed to a conference report is not debatable and cannot be filibustered. The conference report itself is subject to filibuster once the Senate is debating it. Like all legislative filibusters, ending debate requires invoking cloture with a three-fifths vote. If the conference report is rejected by either chamber, the other body is notified. A new conference may be sought.

When both chambers have reached final agreement, an "enrolled" copy—the final official version of the bill or resolution—is printed on parchment and certified by the Secretary of the Senate or the Clerk of the House, depending on which body first passed it. The vice president and Speaker of the House then sign it, and it is delivered to the president for signature or veto.

F. Failure to Take Up a Measure

Especially when the chambers are run by different parties, the prolific House peppers the Senate with legislation, much of which simply dies there. But even under unified party control, many House-passed bills are never taken up in the Senate. The procedural leverage afforded to the minority party and individual senators can slow down the pace of House bills in the Senate and frequently block them entirely. A smaller number of Senate-passed bills meet the same fate in the House.

At times, the knowledge that the Senate minority will prevent a particular bill from advancing encourages passage of legislation in the House, because it amounts to a free pass. Members can vote for legislation without the risk of being held accountable for negative outcomes. This may partially explain the ability of congressional Republicans to call for—and in the House, to adopt—repeal of the Affordable Care Act repeatedly. When they gained control of both chambers in 2015, they were unable to repeat that feat even though the procedure they were using (budget reconciliation) precluded a filibuster in the Senate.

G. The President

When a measure has been approved by the House and Senate, an enrolled copy is transmitted to the president. Article I, Section 7 of the Constitution grants the president ten days, not counting Sundays, to act on a measure once it has been presented. The president may sign the bill or joint resolution into law, allow it to become law without a signature by waiting ten days (excluding Sundays), or veto it and return it to the chamber of origin with written objections, normally referred to as a "veto message."

Congress can override a veto by the president and enact the measure "the objections of the president to the contrary notwithstanding" by a two-thirds vote of members voting, provided a quorum is present, in each chamber. If Congress overrides the measure with the necessary two-thirds votes, it is not returned to the president. The override is certified by the Clerk of the House and the Secretary of the Senate, and the bill is sent to the National Archives as law. If either chamber fails to provide the two-thirds necessary to approve the vetoed measure, the veto is sustained and the measure does not become law.

The president has an alternative course to disapprove a measure, called a "pocket veto." If the Congress adjourns during the ten-day period in which the president must sign the measure, it does not become law and is not returned to the Congress. Such a veto cannot be overridden.

The transmittal of the congressionally enacted bill to the president by the enrolling clerk can be within hours or delayed for weeks. On occasion, this timing may be used strategically to prevent the president from pocket vetoing a bill or resolution by avoiding a period of adjournment. Both the House and the Senate have also, on rare occasion, designated the Clerk of the House or the Secretary of the Senate to receive a vetoed bill from the president, in an effort to block the use of a pocket veto.

Vetoes are difficult for Congress to override. Nonetheless, all presidents other than John Kennedy and Lyndon Johnson have had vetoes overridden.

The threat of a veto from the president usually plays a powerful role in the course of legislation through the Congress. During the drafting process of major legislation, the president often issues a "Statement of Administration Policy" with respect to versions of the bill. SAPs vary in length, but the most significant language is a written notice that the president's advisors would recommend a veto if a bill contains certain provisions. Congress may try to mitigate a veto threat by modifying the contentious provisions.

Sometimes, however, Congress welcomes the battle. Congress may also leverage an expected veto in order to pass a bill and take credit for legislating, without necessarily having to take responsibility for enacting the bill's underlying policy. For instance, a narrow majority in Congress may pass a joint resolution of disapproval to negate some action of a president from the other party. Congress can pass the resolution, the president can veto it, but a closely divided Congress will not be able to override the veto. As a result, the disapproval resolution fails and the executive action remains in place.

When a president vetoes a bill, Congress is not obligated to act. This is usually an indication that the president has the votes to sustain the veto in at least one of the two chambers. Even if one chamber votes to override, the other may decline to take it up.

One power that presidents lack is the "line-item" veto. The line-item veto would permit the president to reject individual items within a bill rather than be required to accept or reject the entire bill. Governors of most states are able to exercise some form of a line-item veto. Presidents of both parties for more than a century have supported some form of line-item veto.

In 1996, Congress enacted a version of the line-item veto that President Clinton signed into law. Clinton used that new power to strike 82 items from 11 different laws. Congress overrode particular line-item vetoes 28 times.

In 1998, the Supreme Court struck down the line-item veto as unconstitutional. Justice John Paul Stevens's majority opinion in *Clinton v. New York* held: "…this act gives the president the unilateral power to change the text of duly enacted statute." He wrote that line-item vetoes of this sort are "the functional equivalent of partial repeals of acts of Congress."

Congress, likewise, cannot "legislatively veto" executive action without the concurrence of the president. Until the early 1980s, Congress delegated authority to the executive branch to take certain actions but retained the ability to overturn those actions, sometimes by a vote of just one chamber. In *INS v. Chadha* (1983), the Supreme Court reviewed a challenge to such a law, and struck down the process as an unconstitutional legislative veto. When Congress legislates, the Court held, the Constitution requires it to follow the formalities of bicameralism and presentment.

Chapter 7
Drafting Legislation

Table of Sections

A. Introduction

A crucial step in passing a law is drafting the legislative text. While only elected officials may formally introduce legislation, they rely extensively on personal office staff, committee professional staff, and nonpartisan legislative counsel to craft the language of bills and accompanying reports. Outside advocates also play important roles. Lobbyists and nongovernmental policy experts can draft significant pieces of bill text, and are well advised to draft legislation carefully and thoroughly before submitting it to members for consideration.

This chapter outlines fundamental principles for writing bill text and report language. For more detailed and advanced drafting guidance, the House and Senate Legislative Counsel offices provide valuable handbooks, many of which are available to the public free of charge. Alumni of those offices have authored and edited comprehensive volumes that are valuable investments for students and practitioners of legislative drafting.

B. Organization of Bill Text

The largest, most complex pieces of legislation are divided into Divisions, Titles, Chapters, and Parts. Below that level, and more relevant to most drafting projects, are "sections" and their constituent parts. Sections are the fundamental building blocks of legislation. Below is a representation of a bill section, with details about how to mark and identify each of its components:

1. Section. Sections are the basic building blocks of legislation. Titles should be clear and straightforward. If the section does not lend itself to division into multiple subsections, text may begin immediately. Introduce sections with Arabic numerals. If a section will sit in a particular title of a larger bill, but its precise position is uncertain, use a construct like "Sec. 2___" to denote placement within that title—in this example, a section within title II of a bill.

(a) **Subsection**. Use subsections when the section divides into two or more major elements. The same rule of division flows through all tiers: a subsection (a) requires at least a subsection (b).

   (1) **Paragraph**. Use Arabic numerals in parentheses for paragraphs.

      (A) **Subparagraph**. Use capital letters in parentheses.

         (i) **Clause**. Use lower-case Roman numerals for clauses. In most pieces of legislation, clauses should be the last level of division.

            (I) **Subclause**. Use capital Roman numerals for subclauses, but use subclauses and "items," led by double lower-case letters in parentheses ("(aa)") sparingly. When a section breaks down into so many parts, it has become quite complex, and drafters should consider whether the text can be rewritten more clearly.

These principles of organization apply to most legislative drafting projects, whether the draft bill is "free-standing" or "amendatory." As the terms suggest, free-standing provisions represent a new piece of law, and amendatory provisions update existing laws.

Within amendatory drafting, drafters should note the technical differences that arise between amending "positive law" provisions of the U.S. Code and amending non-positive statutes. Positive law provisions are those enacted into law as part of the U.S. Code, even if they originated as standalone provisions. Laws that have not (yet) been enacted into positive law are still known by their original enacting vehicle, either its formal name or a short title. The positive vs. non-positive distinction makes little difference in legal effect; both are expressions of federal law.

When amending positive law, drafters direct changes to the relevant section and title of the Code. For instance, section 121 of the Fiscal Year 2024 National Defense Authorization Act ("NDAA") states:

> (a) MODIFICATION OF REQUIREMENTS.—
> > (1) IN GENERAL.—Subsection (e) of section 8062 of title 10, United States Code, is amended to read as follows—
> "(e) The Secretary of the Navy shall ensure that
> > "(1) the Navy maintains a minimum of 9 carrier air wings..."

Here, paragraph (a)(1) of section 121 the NDAA modifies an existing provision in the part of the U.S. Code that governs the military, specifically subsection (e) of section 8062 of title 10. Note the quotation marks preceding the "(e)". That placement signals precisely where the new legislation (i.e., the NDAA) is directing changes to the Code.

When amending non-positive law, drafters direct changes to the earlier free-standing statute. For example, another section of that same NDAA amended the Defense Production Act of 1950 ("DPA"):

> (b) REPORTS ON EXERCISE OF TITLE III AUTHORITIES.—
> Title III of the Defense Production Act of 1950 (50 U.S.C. 4531 et seq.) is amended by adding at the end the following new section:
> "SEC. 305. REPORTS ON EXERCISE OF AUTHORITIES..."

This provision—section 1080 of the NDAA—amends title III of the Defense Production Act itself, not the corresponding section of the U.S. Code—title 50, beginning at section 4351—where the DPA text is reprinted for convenient access.

Organization is key, especially when drafting legislation that amends or updates existing legislation. The "Ramseyer" method (or "Cordon" method, as it is known in the Senate) is a helpful technique to stay organized and analyze the effects of amendatory language. This method shows changes to the underlying law—whether positive or non-positive—by highlighting additions and deletions. Reading the text of an amendatory provision alongside a Ramseyer edit of the underlying text is an excellent way to check drafting work.

C. Substantive Drafting

No matter the subject matter, drafters should start with a clear set of statements to carry out the policy goals of legislation. Most legislation requires an entity to do something, or prohibits an entity from doing something. After establishing that basic requirement, bill text can incorporate definitions, qualifications, exceptions, deadlines, consequences, or sundry other nuances.

Legislative drafters describe statutory "verbs" in four basic categories. Statutes can: require action (typically using the word "shall"); proscribe action (using the phrase "may not"); permit action, without requiring it ("may"); establish legislative facts, definitions, or presumptions, using terms like "means" or "includes"; or set effective dates, either on a particular date or after a certain number of days following the enactment of the legislation. These categories and verbs are basic building blocks of legislation, and they offer helpful starting points for most drafting projects.

Statutes frequently use lists to organize subjects. Lists can be helpful, but drafters should consider the form before writing one. Most statutory lists are either "colon lists" or "dash lists."

Colon lists are introduced by a basic statement and a colon ("(a) The Secretary must take the following actions:"), followed by sub-elements containing the individual directives or prohibitions ("(1) Establish an office; (2) Publish implementation guidance; and (3) Submit an annual report to the committee."). These types of lists can be amended easily, simply by adding a new element and making conforming technical changes.

Dash lists are effectively run-on statutory sentences. They can accomplish similar objectives, but are more useful when drafters do not anticipate adding new elements to the basket of actions that follows the introductory dash.

In either case, drafters must pay careful attention to whether a multi-element test or requirement is conjunctive or disjunctive. The key signal is the word that precedes the last element. "And" establishes a conjunctive test: in a statute that establishes qualifications, for instance, the actor must meet every one of the elements in order to meet the qualification. "Or" establishes a disjunctive test. In that case, the actor could meet any one of the various elements, while failing others, and still meet the qualification.

These are simply examples of the tools available for drafters. Substantive drafting is a craft that benefits from practice, revision, feedback, and subject matter expertise. But good legislative writing shares many of the hallmarks of any good writing, and attentive drafters can be confident in their ability to hone these skills.

D. Strategic Considerations

The sheer volume of legislation introduced in every Congress presents a decision for members and drafters: should new bill text stand out, or move quietly in the background? If the goal is publicity, drafters should spend time creating a pithy, memorable title for the bill. Often this is an acronym of the verbose short title. The CARES Act of 2020, for instance, was formally enacted as the "Coronavirus Aid, Relief, and Economic Security Act." The USA PATRIOT Act of 2001 was the "Uniting and Strengthening America by Providing Appropriate Tools Required to Intercept and Obstruct Terrorism Act." Shorthand references allow sponsors and advocates to make crisp references to precise pieces of legislation.

On the other hand, some legislative strategies call for subtlety. In those cases, drafters should choose a title with the most anodyne words that still fairly describe the effect of the legislative language, which itself might be written in technical, inaccessible jargon. A section titled "New Authorities for the Secretary" may take up less than a page of text, but can vastly expand powers or remove obstacles. Drafters can never assume that a statutory provision will go unnoticed forever, but some intentional fog in drafting may buy time for enactment before opponents fully parse the implications of an obscure provision and organize a campaign against it.

At a higher level, drafters should also consider whether bill text or directive report language ("DRL") will best accomplish the policy goals. Each has advantages and disadvantates:

- **Bill Text**

  Advantages

    o As federal law (passed with bicameralism and presentment), it is persistent and legally binding.

    o Can easily establish recurring requirements, without needing annual reenactment.

  Disadvantages

    o Potentially subject to competing jurisdictional claims by committees.

    o Vulnerable to significant amendments, including in conference or in exchanges of amendments between the chambers.

    o Typically faces a longer lag time between introduction and enactment, compared to DRL, which takes effect after a successful committee vote.

    o Before enactment, single-committee bill text can often be downgraded to conference report language ("Statement of Managers" or "Joint Explanatory Statement"), producing a similar outcome to committee DRL, but with the imprimatur of both chambers. This is a frequent outcome for provisions establishing one-time reports or briefings.

- **Directive Report Language (DRL)**

  Advantages

    o Can be carried by either committee without requiring action by the other.

- o Language is typically much more conversational and accessible—an advantage when clarity is a primary objective.

- o Not subject to amendment on floor or in conference.

- o Takes effect once passed by committee—an advantage if timing of a briefing or report is a priority.

Disadvantages

- o Does not carry the force of law; compliance is a matter of custom and comity.

- o Usually cannot establish recurring reporting or briefing requirements.

- o Cannot compel spending, alter existing law, or otherwise enact significant policy changes.

E. Writing with an Eye to Enactment and Review

Legislative text should be clear: a well-drafted statute will not prompt questions or uncertainty in execution and application. Even the most carefully written laws, however, are subject to judicial review. Federal courts have established a robust and extensive body of law related to statutory interpretation. While these rules, principles, and canons are beyond the scope of an introductory primer on legislative drafting, some familiarity with interpretive approaches will help drafters avoid pitfalls.

Drafters must be mindful of how much authority to vest in another branch of government. Congress can certainly repeal or supersede laws, but a federal statute can only be overruled by another statute passed through bicameralism and presentment, or by a constitutional amendment. Congress can certainly give executive officers the discretion to waive provisions or extend deadlines, but may not give them so much authority that it would be a functional abdication of its own constitutional power to legislate. The Supreme Court explained the boundaries of this "non-delegation doctrine" in a series of cases that arose during and after the Great Depression. In one landmark case, it held that "Congress cannot delegate legislative power to the President to exercise an unfettered discretion to make whatever laws he thinks may be needed or advisable." To pass constitutional muster, a statute must have at least an "intelligible principle" to guide executive discretion. As the Court held in another case: "If Congress shall lay down by legislative act an intelligible principle to which the [executive] … is directed to conform, such legislative action is not a forbidden delegation of legislative power." The doctrine has not been widely used to strike down laws since the New Deal era, but it has emerged in recent years in commentary and legal briefs by opponents of the administrative state.

Two other interpretive doctrines have recently increased the importance of detailed legislative drafting. The first pertains to review of ambiguous statutes; the second involves the correlation between the significance of a policy issue and the scale and precision of bill text that addresses it.

For decades, courts followed a series of rules that governed review of agency regulations when the underlying statutory scheme was ambiguous or silent. The judicial approach in those cases was known as "Chevron deference," named for the 1984 case of *Chevron U.S.A. Inc. v. Natural Resources Defense Council*. The review was indeed deferential: an agency's regulation was typically upheld if the statute was silent or ambiguous, and the agency's approach was reasonable.

In 2024, the Court overruled *Chevron*. In *Loper Bright Enterprises v. Raimondo*, it emphasized the judicial duty to assess agency behavior and prohibited courts from deferring to agencies, even in cases of ambiguity or statutory silence. Although the case was as much about the relationship between Congress and the courts as about the relationship between Congress and the executive branch, *Loper Bright* suggests that Congress will have to expend more time and resources in drafting to avoid an interpretive result at odds with its intent. Prior to 2024, some statutes were drafted with significant flexibility in the text, as a product of political compromise. After

Loper Bright, Congress will have a harder time pushing implementation questions to the executive branch and the regulatory process.

In a related development, courts and commentators have held Congress to a high standard of drafting when addressing issues of major national importance. Under the so-called "major questions doctrine," a court can strike down agency action that is not clearly supported by statutory text. The Supreme Court addressed this issue in 2022 in *West Virginia v. Environmental Protection Agency.* The Court held that "in certain extraordinary cases, both separation of powers principles and a practical understanding of legislative intent make us 'reluctant to read into ambiguous statutory text' the delegation claimed to be lurking there. To convince us otherwise, something more than a merely plausible textual basis for the agency action is necessary. The agency instead must point to 'clear congressional authorization' for the power it claims." Courts have not clarified what precisely constitutes a "major" question, but legislative drafters now have additional incentive to write with precision, clarity, and volume.

F. Working with Legislative Counsel

A legislative counsel office exists in both the House and the Senate to assist members and their staff. "Leg [pronounced "*ledge*"] counsel," as they are often called, are lawyers and draftsmen who prepare legislative text on a confidential and nonpartisan basis at the direction of members and staff. Policy objectives are defined by the member through their staff, and legislative counsel help shape the legislative language to accomplish those objectives. This assistance is available to members for drafting bills, resolutions, and amendments.

House and Senate leg counsels follow slightly different drafting conventions. Even non-substantive style differences, such as formatting dates, can prevent provisions from being "mirror images" in a conference committee, so drafters must engage proactively with leg counsel whether the intent is to preserve or eliminate scope for conference negotiations.

The legislative counsel in the Senate is appointed by the president *pro tempore*. In the House, legislative counsel is appointed by the Speaker. Additional attorneys are hired by the legislative counsel in each chamber. These are career, non-partisan positions. These attorneys specialize in particular issue areas and are frequently assigned to work with specific committees. Legislative counsel are bound by a code of professional conduct that governs confidentiality of their drafting. Leg counsel will not, for instance, discuss with committee professional staff any conversations that the counsel may have had with staff in a personal office, even if that member serves on the committee and the legislation is under consideration in committee. They also owe duties of care and diligence that require them to point out potential shortcomings in legislation, including if the legislation is potentially unconstitutional. Ultimately, however, leg counsel will generally accede to the direction of the members, who are responsible for making the political judgment associated with introducing and voting on legislation. Documenting potential concerns allows leg counsel to fulfil their drafting duties consistent with their professional responsibility as attorneys.

Chapter 8
Authorizations, Appropriations, and the Power of the Purse

A. Introduction

Article I of the Constitution imbues Congress with significant power to control taxes, raise revenue, direct the expenditure of funds, and borrow to meet deficits. These authorities form "the power of the purse."

Congress legislates through authorizations, appropriations, and the budget process. Each has a distinct function, but they are interrelated and interdependent.

Some tools enjoy special expedited ("fast-track") procedures to facilitate more efficient progress through Congress and to the president's desk. While fast-track procedures affect both the House and the Senate by imposing time limits on debate, the impact is greatest in the Senate, where debate is otherwise generally unlimited. In some circumstances, the majority has even used fast-track procedures as a loophole to circumvent the Senate filibuster.

B. Authorizations

An authorization is a law that establishes a program or agency and sets the terms and conditions under which it operates. Authorization bills describe what an agency is permitted to or required to do, and may restrict or prohibit actions by an agency.

Authorizations merely provide the authority for discretionary spending through appropriations bills under the jurisdiction of the House and Senate Appropriations Committees. They may authorize spending at levels higher than what the relevant appropriations committee ultimately provides for an agency or program. Those excess authorizations are generally irrelevant, unless they are matched with supplemental appropriations.

Authorization bills can also establish programs under which recipients who meet certain qualifications and criteria are able to receive funds. These are referred to as mandatory spending programs and sometimes as entitlement programs. "Entitlement" refers to the fact that such programs create a requirement to provide the benefits to individuals who qualify under that law.

Except for these entitlement programs, authorization bills generally cannot have direct budgetary impacts. During the drafting process for authorization bills, the Congressional Budget Office will review ("score") the text and estimate budgetary impacts of the legislation. A provision in an authorization bill that scores—meaning that it creates mandatory spending—can present significant challenges for the overall legislation. Authorizing committees typically modify or exclude language in response to a CBO score to safeguard final passage of the bill. Most appropriations are made on an annual basis.

Authorization bills may be permanent or temporary for one or more years. Temoporary authorizations require periodic reauthorization, but politically sensitive programs within a particular authorization can lead Congress to neglect the necessary reauthorization. For example, State Department programs authorized annually under the Foreign Relations Authorization Act were enacted in 2002, expired two years later, and were not reauthorized until December 2016, when Congress passed the Department of State Authorities Act. From 2002 through 2016, Congress avoided working through the many thorny foreign policy issues that would arise in this authorization. By contrast, the National Defense Authorization Act has been enacted into law every year since 1961.

Although appropriations notionally require prior authorization, examples of unauthorized appropriations abound. Often the appropriations bill in question simply waives the applicable requirement. Rules also prohibit legislating on an appropriations bill. In this context, "legislating" refers to language that changes or repeals existing law. However, if points of order are not raised against offending provisions and they become law, there is no legal bar against such provisions even if they originated in an appropriations bill.

C. Appropriations

Appropriations bills allow the federal government to spend money. When passed by Congress and signed by the president, they authorize federal agencies to incur obligations and direct the federal treasury to spend funds. Article I, Section 9 of the Constitution states: "No Money shall be drawn from the Treasury, but in Consequence of Appropriations made by Law..."

The Founders saw this as a limitation on executive power. James Madison explained in *The Federalist* No. 58:

> The House of Representatives cannot only refuse, but they alone can propose the supplies requisite for the support of the government. They, in a word, hold the purse... This power over the purse may, in fact, be regarded as the most complete and effectual weapon with which any constitution can arm the immediate representatives of the people, for obtaining a redress of every grievance, and for carrying into effect every just and salutary measure.

This limitation lies at the heart of the principle of separation of powers.

The president is required to submit a budget request to the Congress no later than the first Monday in February. As part of that submission, the executive branch provides extensive information assembled by the Office of Management and Budget (OMB) in support of the budgetary proposals the president is making.

Congress considers twelve annual appropriations bills, each handled by a separate subcommittee of the House and Senate Appropriations Committees. Since the first Congress, most appropriations have been provided for no more than a single year, necessitating an annual process.

There are three types of appropriations bills:

- *Regular appropriations bills* provide funding to agencies for the upcoming governmental fiscal year, which runs from October 1 through September 30.

- *Supplemental appropriations bills* provide additional funding during the fiscal year when regular appropriations prove insufficient. Common reasons for a supplemental appropriation include recovery from natural disasters and to fund military actions not anticipated in the regular budget.

- *Continuing resolutions (CRs)* are joint resolutions that provide stopgap funding for agencies when regular appropriations bills have not been enacted into law by the beginning of the fiscal year. CRs often extend funding at the same level as the previous year, but may also increase or reduce it. In some cases, they adopt the lower amount from either a House- or Senate-passed regular appropriations bill. CRs are in effect for a fixed period— sometimes a matter of days during negotiations to pass the regular appropriations bills, at other times much longer, weeks or months. In some years, a CR has been necessary to provide funding for the entire fiscal year.

Executive branch agencies are severely constrained under a CR. Their funding is reduced in real terms because of the effect of inflation, and they generally cannot initiate new starts of programs that were not underway in the preceding fiscal year. Congress can grant "anomalies" for particular programs in CRs, but those exceptions are rare and politically volatile. Outside lobbyists are almost always unsuccessful in requesting anomalies in connection with a CR.

In some years, Congress has failed to enact some or all of the regular appropriations bills and instead opted to combine multiple bills into a single measure. These are referred to as omnibus appropriations bills. Omnibus bills are often considered late in the year, on the cusp of recess or adjournment. As a result, members often complain they have insufficient time to study these massive bills. Some members who otherwise might support the provisions contained in an omnibus bill feel compelled to vote against it in opposition to the procedure. Smaller omnibus bills with just a few regular appropriations bills combined are sometimes labeled "minibus" bills.

Before the House or Senate Appropriations Committees act on an appropriations bill, their subcommittees conduct extensive oversight and markups, guided by spending allocations provided under the budget resolution. The Appropriations Committee in each chamber receives a single allocation set out in the statement of managers that accompanies the conference report on the budget resolution, known as the "302(a) allocation." The Appropriations Committee chair divides that amount into separate allocations, one for each of its subcommittees. These are known as the "302(b) sub-allocations."

In both chambers, appropriations bills are prepared and marked up in subcommittee. While the full committee may mark the bill up further, the subcommittee's work is often decisive.

In the House, appropriations bills are privileged for floor consideration. Although they do not require a special rule, they typically come to the floor under one that waives points of order against appropriating funds for programs not previously authorized.

If the necessary appropriations are not enacted into law by the end of the fiscal year or before a continuing resolution expires, government agencies that have not been funded must cease operations. Shutdowns are required under the Antideficiency Act of 1884, which prohibits federal agencies from obligating or expending federal funds without or in excess of an appropriation.

Government shutdowns in recent years have been a consequence of disagreements between the president and the opposition party in the Congress. It has become routine for Congress to fail to complete the necessary twelve appropriations bills by the end of the fiscal year. The last time all twelve appropriations bills became law prior to the beginning of the next fiscal year was in 1996. This has frequently emboldened both parties to use the impending upheaval of a government shutdown as powerful leverage in appropriations negotiations.

D. 1974 Budget Act

The Congressional Budget and Impoundment Control Act was enacted on July 12, 1974, and signed by President Richard Nixon. Beginning with the Budget and Accounting Act of 1921, the budgeting process had been dominated by the executive branch, as that law gave the president a formal role in the development of the federal budget for the first time. It required the president to submit an annual budget request to Congress before it considered appropriations and revenue legislation, and it created the Bureau of the Budget, later reorganized as the Office of Management and Budget (OMB) in 1971.

Prior to 1974, Congress made appropriations decisions on individual spending bills and revenue decisions on individual tax bills without systematically considering how the overall budget was affected. Bills were passed and signed into law and it was not until the end of the fiscal year that the size of the deficit or surplus became clear.

For much of U.S. history—except during World War II—deficits and surpluses were small enough that the system seemed to work. But rising annual deficits in the early 1970s made a more comprehensively planned and reasoned approach to budgetary decisions increasingly necessary.

In 1974, political will and opportunity aligned. Two important contributing factors led to the passage of the Congressional Budget and Impoundment Act. First, President Nixon refused to spend approximately $12 billion (more than $78 billion in 2025 dollars) in funding that had been appropriated by Congress using a procedure called impoundment.

Virtually every prior president throughout U.S. history had impounded funds. However, the amounts involved were minimal, congressional appropriators were generally consulted, and there were good reasons for declining to spend the funds (for example, a program was no longer needed). Nixon's impoundments were not small, were not agreed to by Congress, and his reasons were controversial. He declared that it was the "constitutional right for the President of the United States to impound funds." He pledged,

"I will not spend money if the Congress overspends..."

Many in Congress saw impoundment as presidential usurpation of Congress's control of the purse strings. As this confrontation wore on, it provided some of the impetus for Congress to act. But perhaps most importantly, President Nixon's political standing was weak as he was absorbed by the Watergate crisis. The Congressional Budget and Impoundment Control Act was overwhelmingly adopted by the House (401-6) and unanimously adopted in the Senate (95-0) in June 1974. Nixon signed it in July; a month later he resigned.

The Act provided a means for Congress to coordinate and enhance its control over the annual budget and it reduced the ability of presidents to impound funds. Among other things, the Act created the Congressional Budget Office (CBO) to provide independent budget analysis to Congress, ending the executive branch's near domination of budgetary information. Congress would no longer be dependent on the executive branch Office of Management and Budget (OMB), which is within the Executive Office of the President.

Among the major assumptions at the time of the enactment of the law was that the new budget process would be largely bipartisan. The battles over appropriations, entitlement programs, and tax legislation could take place within an agreed upon budgetary framework. Also, it was thought that deficits would be reduced by the new procedures since Congress would be required to explicitly vote on them.

Both of these assumptions turned out to be wrong. Almost without exception, when the annual budget resolution comes to the Senate floor, the vote is close to straight party line. Because the expedited procedures under which the resolution is considered reduces the leverage of the minority in the Senate, the majority can bypass the minority and adopt its budget proposal. It is similar in the House. The process envisioned as a way to temper partisanship has instead contributed to the acceleration and broadening of partisan polarization in the Congress.

Second, the budget process has not effectively restrained annual deficits. As we will see, at times budget procedures are used to adopt proposals that greatly increase the deficit.

The provisions of the Act that created legislative procedures were enacted under the rulemaking authority of Congress. As such, these provisions of the Budget Act are similar to House and Senate rules, in that either chamber is able to amend those provisions that affect its operations without the concurrence of the other chamber and without the enactment of a law.

One unusual provision in the Budget Act applies to Senate consideration of both the Congressional Budget Resolution and reconciliation bills: while total debate time is limited (50 hours for the budget resolution and 20 hours for reconciliation), there is no limit on the number of amendments that can be offered. This creates a situation in which a large stack of amendments are voted on after all debate has expired, a process known as a "vote-a-rama," which often takes many hours, sometimes stretching over two days.

E. The Congressional Budget Resolution

The heart of the process created by the Budget Act is the requirement that Congress pass a concurrent resolution each year known as the Congressional Budget Resolution. This required budget resolution is privileged for consideration and adoption, meaning it can't be filibustered. As a concurrent resolution (numbered as H. Con. Res. xx or S. Con. Res. xx), it must be adopted in identical form by both houses, but it is not sent to the president and does not become law. It creates a binding budget "blueprint" that Congress is expected to follow as it makes spending and revenue decisions—though, as with almost any rule Congress imposes on itself, it may choose to set it aside.

The president is required by law to submit a comprehensive budget request to Congress on or after the first Monday in January, but no later than the first Monday in February, although it frequently arrives late. This request is a detailed proposal for all federal programs, accompanied by multiple volumes of tables, charts, legislative proposals, and supporting documents. It includes estimated receipts, expenditures, and proposed appropriations for the following five fiscal years, although some presidents have submitted ten-year budgets.

Once the president has developed a budget request and presented it to Congress, the congressional budget process begins. The law requires that this be done on or before the first Monday in February, although that date often slips. Budget decisions are made on the basis of the federal fiscal year; since 1974, the federal fiscal year begins on October 1 and ends on September 30. The law sets forth a timetable for each procedural step along the way to the adoption of the budget resolution.

The Senate Budget Committee must report the budget resolution by April 1. The law contains no similar deadline for the House Budget Committee. There are consequences if the Senate Budget Committee fails to meet this deadline. Specifically, should that deadline pass, budget resolutions submitted by individual senators are considered referred to and discharged from the Budget Committee and placed on the Senate calendar. Under these conditions, such individual budget resolutions are privileged for consideration.

The law stipulates that the budget resolution must be adopted by Congress by April 15. However, budget resolutions have rarely been completed by this date, and in multiple years, no resolution was adopted at all.

Procedures related to the timetable established by the Budget Act are enforced in both chambers by points of order. In the House, these may be waived by a special rule. In the Senate, points of order may be waived by majority vote, with the exception of a prohibition against the Senate acting on any appropriations measures until the Appropriations Committee has established the spending caps for each of its subcommittees (called sub-allocations). That process requires a three-fifths vote.

The Budget Act requires that the budget resolution establish budget aggregates and spending levels for each broad functional category of the budget (for example, national defense, energy, health, natural resources and environment, and Medicare). The aggregates include:

- total revenues (and the amount by which the total is to be changed by legislative action);
- total new budget authority and outlays;
- the deficit or surplus; and
- the debt limit.

The budget resolution does not allocate funds among specific programs. However, it is common in floor debate (and sometimes in the Budget Committee report) to detail "assumptions" underlying the totals for budget functions. These assumptions are not binding. Yet members frequently frame such assumptions as if they were substantive changes affecting specific line items in the budget. For example, an amendment to increase the Education, Training, Employment, and Social Services function by $200 million, may be referred to by its supporters as a $200 million increase in "special education." This is the assumption of the sponsors, but the additional funding may ultimately be spent through an appropriation on some other purpose within the budget function.

F. Reconciliation Bills

The 1974 law also set up a second, optional procedure known as budget reconciliation. Reconciliation is a powerful tool when one party controls both chambers of Congress and the presidency. It unfolds in two stages: first the budget resolution includes reconciliation instructions. Second, a reconciliation bill is enacted to change laws affecting spending or revenue.

Reconciliation instructions direct committees in the House and Senate to report changes in current law regarding revenues and entitlement spending. These instructions specify the dollar amount of the increase or reduction, but the committee of jurisdiction determines how to achieve the change.

If more than one committee receives reconciliation instructions, the recommendations reported by those committees are assembled by the House and Senate Budget Committees into one bill. Under the Congressional

Budget and Impoundment Control Act of 1974, neither the House nor the Senate Budget Committee can amend the recommendations submitted to it.

Although reconciliation bills under the Congressional Budget and Impoundment Control Act of 1974 receive expedited consideration in both chambers, it is in the Senate where the most dramatic procedural effects of reconciliation, and consequently the most controversial impacts, occur.

Debate in the Senate on reconciliation measures is limited to twenty hours, making filibusters impossible. Cloture is therefore unnecessary to end debate, and a simple majority, rather than the usual three-fifths supermajority (normally 60 votes), suffices to end debate and pass the bill. In addition, unlike normal Senate rules, the Congressional Budget and Impoundment Control Act of 1974 requires that all amendments considered on a reconciliation bill be germane. (Germaneness is a requirement that an amendment be closely related to the precise subject of the text it proposes to amend.)

When reconciliation is used for its legitimate deficit reduction purpose, another special requirement applies: amendments must not cause a committee to fall short of its reconciliation instruction. Unless a committee has recommended savings in excess of its instruction, this means that amendments must be deficit-neutral. In practice, this means that any spending increase must be offset by an equal spending cut or revenue increase, and any revenue reduction must be offset by revenue increases or entitlements cuts of the same amount.

The House is not impacted in the same way because it legislates under a special rule reported by the Rules Committee. On reconciliation, the special rule generally expedites the process by limiting debate, amendments, and other action, but this is not outside of the House's normal procedures.

The drafters of the reconciliation process expected it to be used to make minor adjustments in spending and tax bills passed earlier in the year to bring them in line with the budget resolution. The aggressive use of reconciliation as a way to work around the Senate filibuster rules to pass major sweeping legislation was not contemplated in 1974.

Beginning in 1981, however, Congress began using reconciliation bills in a significant way to implement policies laid out in the budget resolution. In 1996, the Clinton Administration used the process to push welfare reform through Congress. In 2003, President George W. Bush employed it to secure major tax cuts, with Vice President Cheney casting the deciding vote. Measures like these, which served to increase the deficit or enact major non-budgetary provisions, were also not envisioned by the authors of the congressional budget process in 1974. In recent Congresses, constraints on reconciliation have weakened further, with both parties enacting spending priorities in reconciliation bills that ordinarily would be categorized as discretionary appropriations. These liminal cases illustrate the tensions that arise within Congress even when a party has unified control: appropriators are loath to surrender their spending power, even when party leadership exerts pressure to exploit reconciliation.

The principal attraction of reconciliation remains its ability to circumvent the Senate filibuster. Debate is strictly limited on a reconciliation bill under the Congressional Budget and Impoundment Control Act of 1974, so a filibuster is precluded and a simple majority can pass the reconciliation bill. This framework enables the majority to act on major legislation without any input from the minority.

G. The "Byrd Rule" and "Byrd Baths"

By 1985, it had become clear that the reconciliation process created in the Congressional Budget and Impoundment Control Act of 1974 was being increasingly used to circumvent the regular rules of the Senate, particularly the filibuster. At the urging of Minority Leader Robert Byrd—who had been one of the authors of the reconciliation provisions in the 1974 Act— the Senate acted to curb non-budgetary matters in reconciliation bills by creating a new point of order, commonly referred to as the "Byrd Rule." Senator Byrd declared:

> It was never foreseen that the Budget Reform Act would be used in that way. So if the budget reform process is going to be preserved, and

more importantly if we are going to preserve the deliberative process in this U.S. Senate—which is the outstanding, unique element with respect to the U.S. Senate, action must be taken now to stop this abuse of the budget process.

Byrd's concerns were shared by other senators, and his 1985 amendment, which prohibits provisions that do not have an impact on the budget, was adopted 96-0. It has been extended and modified a number of times, and in 1990 it was enacted as a permanent part of the Congressional Budget Act (CBA).

The Byrd Rule has had a significant impact because an effort to waive the rule requires a three-fifths vote of all senators (60 votes in the absence of vacancies). If a point of order under the Byrd Rule is sustained, the offending provision is struck from the bill, or if made against an amendment, the amendment falls. In this way, if a provision is found to violate the Byrd Rule and the rule is not waived, the advantage gained by use of the reconciliation process (the circumvention of the supermajority requirement under cloture) is negated.

The rule is quite complex. However, it can be characterized as prohibiting "extraneous matter" from reconciliation bills. The Byrd Rule provides a six-part definition of extraneous matter as any provision that:

1. does not produce a change in spending or revenues;

2. was recommended by a committee that produces a spending increase or revenue reduction while that committee is not in compliance with its reconciliation instruction;

3. is outside of the jurisdiction of the committee that produced it;

4. produces a change in spending or revenues that is merely incidental to the non-budgetary parts of the provision;

5. would increase the deficit for a year beyond the budget period covered by the reconciliation bill; or

6. recommends changes in Social Security.

While the problem of extraneous material in reconciliation is acute in the Senate because of the availability of the filibuster under the normal Senate rules, the House sometimes addresses extraneous matters by including a prohibition in a special rule.

To ensure compliance, the majority leadership and senators seeking to amend a reconciliation bill typically meet with the Senate parliamentarian to learn in advance whether legislative language will pass muster with the Byrd Rule. These extensive and multiple sessions are referred to as "Byrd baths."

A Byrd Rule point of order has the unusual effect of striking individual provisions from a bill while allowing the rest of the bill to be considered. At times, this feature of the Byrd Rule has been a barrier—intended at least by Senator Byrd—to the use of reconciliation for sweeping authorizing legislation like the Affordable Care Act in 2010 or the efforts to fully repeal it in 2017.

It is a widely held misconception that the reconciliation process was used to enact Obamacare. Early on some Democrats advocated the use of the reconciliation process to pass the bill in order to lower the threshold from 60 to a simple majority (51 if all senators are voting). However, the Democratic leadership, based on strong advice from the Senate parliamentarian and Senator Byrd himself, knew that the legislation contained many non-budgetary items needed to set up an entirely new health insurance system.

Ultimately, the Affordable Care Act was adopted in the Senate under regular rules with 60 Democratic votes (to invoke cloture under Rule XXII) overcoming a filibuster. In the end, a targeted reconciliation bill, the Health Care and Education Reconciliation Act of 2010, carefully scrubbed to ascertain compliance with the Byrd Rule, was used to strike several budgetary provisions from the ACA to make it more acceptable to the House.

H. PAYGO

In 1990, concern about the long-term impact of mandatory (entitlement) spending or tax cuts prompted Congress to enact a new budget rule popularly called "PAYGO," or pay-as-you-go. These processes and limits on discretionary spending were established under the Budget Enforcement Act of 1990 and codified in the Statutory Pay-As-You-Go Act of 2010. PAYGO requires that increases in mandatory spending—because they have on-going impacts on the deficit in future years—must be offset by reductions in mandatory spending elsewhere in the budget or by tax increases. Similarly, tax cuts projected to reduce revenue in future years are required to be "paid for" by increases in other taxes or reductions in entitlement spending.

The 1990 PAYGO provision was "sunsetted," or ended, at the end of fiscal year 2002. Although it was replaced by a series of House and Senate rules that were less effective (confusingly also referred to as PAYGO), statutory PAYGO rules were reestablished in 2010; this version of "S-PAYGO" was enacted on a permanent basis.

Under the new PAYGO rules, the budgetary effects of mandatory spending and tax provisions enacted into law are tracked on a rolling five-year and ten-year basis monitored by the Office of Management and Budget (OMB). At the end of the year if the scorecards for either of these periods shows the effect would be an increase in the deficit, the president must issue a sequestration order requiring across-the-board cuts to non-exempt mandatory spending programs.

 Some programs are exempt from PAYGO sequestration. Social Security, unemployment insurance, Medicaid, and other social safety net programs such as the Supplemental Nutrition Assistance Program are exempt, which increases the severity of the impact of sequestration on programs that are not exempt. Another major exemption is "emergency spending." Administrations have used emergency supplemental bills to finance defense spending under the emergency characterization.

PAYGO does not affect deficit increases arising from changes in mandatory spending or revenues that are projected to occur under existing law. Sequestration under PAYGO has also been avoided through laws instructing OMB to ignore increases in the deficit for that year.

I. Debt Ceiling

Congress must periodically act to raise the "debt ceiling," the statutory cap on how much the federal government can borrow to finance the national debt. The ceiling has existed in law since 1918.

When the limit is reached, additional borrowing cannot occur, which would eventually lead the federal government to default on its debts. Actual default has never occurred, but the brinksmanship associated with debt ceiling negotiations has brought the country close to it. U.S. Treasury bonds are considered among the safest investments by private borrowers and foreign governments. Defaulting on these obligations would raise the cost of borrowing for the government, severely impact the U.S. economy, and likely create upheaval in financial markets.

Both parties have treated the debt ceiling as a political football. Since public understanding of the debt limit is limited, it has been easy for politicians to suggest that lifting the debt ceiling is a way of increasing debt. However, the debt in question is typically already obligated and it's more a question of the government's ability to meet its debts.

The opposition party to the president, by threatening an imminent default, attempts to gain concessions. For example, in 2011, the House Republicans refused to cooperate in lifting the ceiling unless President Obama would agree to significant cuts in federal spending. The 2011 debt limit episode was resolved on August 2, 2011, when President Obama signed the Budget Control Act of 2011 (BCA). The BCA included provisions aimed at deficit reduction and allowing the debt limit to rise in three stages, the latter two subject to congressional disapproval. Once the BCA was enacted, a presidential certification triggered a $400 billion increase. A second certification led to a $500 billion increase on September 22, 2011, and a third, $1,200 billion increase took place on January 28, 2012.

While the crisis was averted, the near miss it involved led to a downgrade of the nation's credit rating. In August 2011, Standard & Poor's, one of the nation's largest credit rating agencies, stripped the U.S. of its AAA status. S&P warned, "The political brinksmanship of recent months highlights what we see as America's governance and policymaking becoming less stable, less effective, and less predictable than what we previously believed. The statutory debt ceiling and the threat of default have become political bargaining chips in the debate over fiscal policy."

Similar battles recurred at regular intervals throughout the 2010s and 2020s. To date, the debt ceiling has always been lifted when necessary.

J. Earmarks

One of the most controversial aspects of the appropriations process has been the use—and subsequent banning—of certain targeted expenditures known as "earmarks."

Definitions of earmarks vary. Even the Congressional Research Service (CRS) has had difficulty developing an all-inclusive and effective definition. OMB used a definition that characterized any expenditure of funds on a specific project not requested by the president as an earmark. Viewed through the lens of checks and balances, this is clearly an executive branch-centric view of earmarks. Presidents frequently embed earmarks in their budget requests.

An earmark is a provision in an appropriations bill, or under some circumstances an authorization bill, or a tax expenditure contained in a revenue bill, focused on a specific program or project requested by a member or members of Congress or in the president's budget request. Earmarks typically benefit a single entity or category of recipient. For example, a provision that increases spending for a light rail grant program might not be an earmark, but a provision that requires an airport exactly 7 miles from the center of a city to receive 20% of the light rail funding would likely be labeled an earmark.

Although earmarks became controversial for a number of reasons, one was the concern about unnecessary spending during a period of large federal deficits. Most earmarks, however, targeted a portion of an existing appropriation prioritizing the specified use, but not increasing the deficit. In reality, earmarks at their peak accounted for about one percent of the budget.

Often, earmarks were not written in statutory language, but appeared in committee reports or statements of managers accompanying conference reports. A famous example came in 2005, when a $223 million earmark in a highway bill funded the construction of a bridge in Alaska from Ketchikan to a nearby island that had only about 50 residents, and the Ketchikan airport. Dubbed the "bridge to nowhere," it became a symbol of earmark excess.

From 2007–2010, both chambers responded to concerns about earmark abuses by inserting them into bills at the last moment with rules increasing transparency. For example, Senate Rule XLIV, adopted in 2007, requires that a "congressionally directed spending item, limited tax benefit, and limited tariff benefit [earmarks], if any, in [a] bill or joint resolution, or in [a] committee report accompanying the bill or joint resolution" be identified through "lists, charts, or other similar means including the name of each Senator who submitted a request to the committee for each item so identified." Senate Rule XLIV also requires that this information be "available on a publicly accessible congressional website in a searchable format at least 48 hours before such vote."

Nevertheless, in 2011, both the House and Senate party caucuses imposed a ban on earmarks. Some observers contend that banning earmarks removes decision-making from elected members of Congress and shifts it to the executive branch. The ban had the effect of taking a relatively public process, at least after the reforms, and making it less transparent. Some refer to "phonemarks" and "lettermarks" to characterize the ability of appropriations committee members and others to deal directly with federal agencies to target funding to programs and projects they favor. This is particularly effective for the members of appropriations subcommittees that control the budget of the agency in question. Another negative impact has been the dismantling of a tool historically used by leadership to negotiate, bargain, and put together support for legislation. Some cite the earmark ban as removing a process that often enhanced and encouraged bipartisanship.

In the 2020s, Congress revived a process to appropriate funds specifically for individual projects. Known as "congressionally directed spending" or "community project funding," these initiatives are functionally equivalent to earmarks, but subject to heightened requirements for disclosure, transparency, and reporting by the Government Accountability Office.

K. Impoundment and Rescissions

The Congressional Budget and Impoundment Control Act of 1974 reformed how presidents may impound appropriated funds. An impoundment is the withholding (or delay), usually by the president, of funds provided for in appropriations. A federal agency can also impound funds by failing to spend the appropriations allocated to it for a given fiscal year.

The Budget and Impoundment Act divides impoundment into "deferrals," which delay the use of funds, and "rescissions," which are requests by the president that Congress cancel an appropriation. A rescission requires that the president submit a specific request to the Congress. More than one rescission can be listed in a request. Congress has a period of 45 days of "continuous session" during which it may approve the rescissions in whole or in part. If Congress fails to act, the president is compelled to spend the funds for the purpose for which it was appropriated.

A deferral also requires a specific request to Congress from the president. Deferrals are limited to purposes listed by the Antideficiency Act; for example, providing for contingencies or achieving savings through greater efficiency. The president cannot defer funding for policy reasons (for example, to cut overall federal spending or because of opposition to a particular program).

Chapter 9

Other Congressional Powers and Relationships with the Executive and Judicial Branches

A. Introduction

In addition to its legislative powers under Article I, Congress has several other constitutional obligations. Article V places Congress at the heart of the process of amending the Constitution. This far-reaching power, shared with the states, does not involve a role for the president.

Some of Congress's most important functions are contained in Article II, which created the Executive Branch. For example, Article II, Section 2 conveys to the president the power to nominate "with the Advice and Consent of the Senate" ambassadors, judges, and executive branch officials, and to make treaties, again subject to "the Advice and Consent of the Senate." The responsibilities to concur in the ratification of treaties and particularly the obligation to participate in the appointment of federal judges have been at the center of considerable political debate in recent years.

Two other activities of importance are oversight and investigations. Congress uses its oversight power to guide the performance of the executive branch and the private sector in carrying out and complying with laws. Congress also has significant power to investigate matters alleging abuse of power, wrongdoing, negligence, or malfeasance.

Article III gives the Congress important duties with respect to the judiciary. Congress may establish or disestablish federal courts other than the Supreme Court and determine the jurisdiction of federal courts, short of limiting the Supreme Court's original jurisdiction.

This chapter also discusses the responsibility given to the House to impeach a president, when warranted, and the power to remove that president by trial in the Senate. Under the Twenty-Fifth Amendment, Congress may also play an important role in the removal of the president. Additionally, Congress counts and certifies electoral ballots in presidential elections, and has the authority to legislate a line of succession to the presidency.

B. Nominations

The Constitution provides for shared power between the president and the Senate with respect to nominations to high executive offices and to all federal judicial nominations. Congress may also determine whether lower level executive nominations require Senate confirmation.

There are more than 1,200 executive branch positions that currently require Senate confirmation, including department heads (such as secretaries, deputy secretaries, under secretaries, and general counsels), leaders of independent agencies (such as administrators and deputy administrators), and members of various boards and commissions. Presidential appointments of U.S. attorneys and U.S. marshals must also be confirmed by the Senate.

Every four years, following presidential elections, the Senate and the House alternate in publishing a book-length listing of politically appointed positions entitled *Policy and Supporting Positions*, more popularly known as the "Plum Book." Printed by the Government Publishing Office, the Plum Book is named for its original cover color, although appreciated for the double meaning.

The Senate alone, chosen by the Framers with stability in mind, shares the power to appoint judges and executive branch officials with the president. The House occasionally plays a role in nominations, if nominees require special legislation to be eligible to serve. For example, federal law prohibits a retired flag officer or general officer from serving as Secretary of Defense "within 10 years after relief from active duty." As of 2025, three retired generals—George Marshall, Jim Mattis, and Lloyd Austin—have been nominated within the restricted time period. In each case, special legislation passed by both chambers and signed by the president allowed the individuals to serve, notwithstanding the general prohibition.

The confirmation process for presidential nominations begins in the committee of jurisdiction over the agency involved: for example, all ambassadors and the Secretary of State would be considered in the Senate Foreign Relations Committee, the Attorney General in the Judiciary

Committee, and the Secretary of Defense in the Armed Services Committee. Committees hold hearings to evaluate the qualifications of the nominees. Nominees, supporters, and opponents may testify, and senators use these opportunities to extract commitments from nominees to take certain actions, if confirmed. For example, chairs or other members of the committee will often seek a commitment that the nominee will agree to testify before the committee when requested to do so. This hearing process plays an important role in facilitating congressional oversight of the executive branch.

Nominations may be reported favorably, unfavorably, or without recommendation to the full Senate by a simple majority vote of the committee. Senate Rule XXVI, paragraph 7(a) requires that a physical majority of the committee be present when this recommendation is made and that a majority of those present approve the recommendation.

A nomination reported to the Senate is placed on the Executive Calendar. The Senate considers nominations in executive session, as opposed to legislative session. The Senate proceeds to executive session by motion or unanimous consent to take up nominations or treaties on the Executive Calendar. By precedent, the motion to proceed to executive session to consider a specified nomination, wherever it may be among the nominations listed on the calendar, is not debatable. As of 2025, executive branch nominations may be called up *en bloc*. Nominations that have not been acted upon when the Senate adjourns or recesses for more than 30 days, or when it adjourns *sine die*, are returned to the president.

When a nomination is called up, the presiding officer poses the question, "Will the Senate advise and consent to this nomination?" The nomination is confirmed by simple majority vote, a quorum being present.

For much of its history, filibusters of nominations in the Senate were rare. In more recent years, as partisanship in the body has increased, it has become more common for the opposition party to oppose some presidential nominations.

Supreme Court nominations are particularly high profile, and the mere possibility of a filibuster often has had some effect on the president's nomination decision in the first place. Because of the supermajority (60 vote) requirement to invoke cloture, presidents anticipated that their nominee would likely require some votes from the opposition party, causing them to avoid some nominees. The same occurred with circuit court and district court nominees, but often in a less publicized fashion.

This changed beginning in 2013 when Senate Majority Leader Harry Reid (D-NV) employed the parliamentary tactic that had been called the "nuclear option." The majority Democrats were successful in establishing the precedent that the words of Senate Rule XXII—ending debate requires a vote of "three-fifths of the Senators duly chosen and sworn"—was to be understood to require only a simple majority on all executive branch nominees and all judicial nominees below the level of the Supreme Court.

Matters escalated in the last year of President Obama's second term. In February 2016, Justice Antonin Scalia died unexpectedly. Within hours of the news breaking, Majority Leader Mitch McConnell vowed that the Senate would not take up any nomination that the president might make, stating, "The American people should have a voice in the selection of their next Supreme Court Justice. Therefore, this vacancy should not be filled until we have a new president."

President Obama ignored the majority leader's advice that he make no nomination, and on March 16, he nominated Judge Merrick Garland to the seat. Backed by the Senate majority and Judiciary Committee Chair Chuck Grassley, the majority leader stonewalled the Garland nomination. After President Trump's election and inauguration, he nominated Judge Neil Gorsuch.

Democrats launched a filibuster of the Gorsuch nomination. With only 52 Republican senators at the time, it was unlikely that the 60 votes necessary for cloture could be reached. Majority Leader McConnell eventually used the same parliamentary tactic that his Democratic predecessor, Harry Reid (D-NV), had used to create a Senate precedent reinterpreting the language of Rule XXII as requiring only a simple majority to end debate by invoking cloture, extending its effect to Supreme Court nominees. This was the so-called nuclear option.

Leader McConnell later refined the justification for the Garland precedent after Justice Ruth Bader Ginsburg died in September 2020, even closer to a presidential election. President Trump nominated Judge Amy Coney Barrett to replace Justice Ginsburg, and the Senate confirmed her elevation just weeks before election day.

The changes in the Senate's interpretation of the number of votes needed to invoke cloture means that a president, if their party holds a majority in the Senate, will only require the support of their own party to confirm judicial nominees to lifetime appointments on the federal courts, including the Supreme Court.

C. Recess Appointments

The president may make temporary appointments during a Senate recess without advice and consent. Article II, Section 2 of the Constitution provides that "The President shall have Power to fill up all Vacancies that may happen during the Recess of the Senate, by granting Commissions which shall expire at the End of their next Session."

This clause originally ensured that government agencies could continue to function during periods when Congress was not in session and therefore the Senate was unavailable to confirm presidential nominees. In earlier periods, Congresses sometimes met for only a few months each year and recesses could be quite extended. Also, travel to and from the capital was slow and unreliable.

Presidents have long used recess appointments to circumvent Senate advice and consent requirements. This occurs typically for political reasons when a nominee is controversial and may be blocked in the Senate.

The use of the Recess Appointments Clause is controversial when it is used to place judges on the federal bench. Unlike other executive branch nominees whose recess appointments end at the expiration of the congressional session, Article III of the Constitution ensures that judges hold life tenure, removable only through impeachment (they "shall hold their Offices during good Behaviour"). The practice is relatively rare, given the serious constitutional questions that arise. To date, the Supreme Court has not opined on the constitutionality of recess appointments to the federal bench.

Recesses fall into two categories: "intrasession" recesses are held within a congressional session, and "intersession" recesses fall between sessions, in the period between the *sine die* adjournment of one session and the convening of the next. Presidents have made recess appointments during each. For much of its history the interpretation of the Recess Appointments Clause was unsettled. Controversy intensified in the modern era.

In 2007, Senate Majority Leader Harry Reid pioneered the use of "pro forma sessions" to block President George W. Bush from making recess appointments during the last years of his administration. Pro forma sessions are sessions in which little or no business occurs in either chamber, but it's the Senate that is relevant here. The presiding officer gavels the body into session and typically immediately gavels the session to a close, in most cases in less than a minute. Usually, only one senator is present. A 1993 Department of Justice memo argued that the president could make a recess appointment during any recess of more than three days. Therefore, Reid argued, by holding a pro forma session of the Senate every three days, the Senate would technically not be in recess. Since the Senate was not in recess, no recess appointment could be made by the president. When the Republicans regained control of the Senate and were interested in blocking recess appointments by President Obama, Majority Leader Mitch McConnell adopted the Reid pro forma session strategy.

In 2012, during an intrasession recess, President Obama made recess appointments of three members to the National Labor Relations Board and a director for the Consumer Financial Protection Bureau, a new agency, ignoring the fact that the Senate was holding pro forma sessions. He argued that "the President may determine that pro forma sessions at which no business is to be conducted do not interrupt a Senate recess for the purposes of the Recess Appointments Clause." Republicans challenged that interpretation.

In 2014, the battle reached the Supreme Court. In a 9-0 decision in *National Labor Relations Board v. Noel Canning*, the Court held that President Obama exceeded his Constitutional authority by making the appointments: "We conclude that we cannot ignore these pro forma sessions… Thus we conclude that the president lacked the power to make the recess appointments…" The Court expanded the number of days required to trigger qualification as a recess under the Recess Appointment Clause from three to ten. In summary, the Court also held: "For purposes of the Recess Appointments Clause, the Senate is in session when it says that it is."

On some occasions the Senate has been forced into pro forma sessions by the House of Representatives. Article I, Section 5 of the Constitution stipulates that neither chamber may recess for more than three days without the approval of the other. By withholding their approval for the necessary concurrent resolution to allow the Senate to adjourn, the House assures that the Senate will conduct at least pro forma sessions, preventing recess appointments by the president even when the Senate majority is aligned with the president.

D. Treaties

The president negotiates treaties with other nations. A treaty may be bilateral, with one other nation, like the two Panama Canal Treaties signed in 1977 with Panama, or multilateral, as with the North Atlantic Treaty that established NATO, signed in 1949 with 11 other founding nations.

Once the president has negotiated and signed a treaty, it is submitted to the Senate and referred to the Foreign Relations Committee. Treaties submitted to the Senate are initially secret under Senate Rule XXIX. The Senate must act to remove the injunction of secrecy. In most cases, this occurs by unanimous consent at the time the treaty is referred to the committee. The committee generally holds hearings, receiving testimony from the administration, other outside experts, opponents of the treaty, and its proponents.

The committee may decide to take no action on the treaty, or it may report the treaty to the full Senate favorably, unfavorably, or without recommendation, at which time it is placed on the Senate's Executive Calendar. The committee generally also submits a written report, known as an executive report.

The Foreign Relations Committee also reports a recommended resolution of ratification, in the form of a Senate Resolution, which is the actual document conveying the Senate's advice and consent. The resolution of ratification may include committee-recommended conditions: proposed amendment to the actual text of the treaty, or proposed reservations, declarations, or understandings that would not change the text of the treaty but would qualify the sentiment of the Senate in advising and consenting to ratification.

Likewise, the actual text of a treaty may be amended on the floor of the Senate, and when consideration of the text of the treaty has been concluded on the Senate floor, the resolution of ratification may also be amended on the floor by the inclusion of reservations.

Reservations are formal declarations that modify the effect of one or more of the provisions of the treaty. The Senate sometimes also includes other additions to the resolution of ratification called "understandings," "interpretations," or "declarations" that do not modify the force of the treaty but are intended to further clarify its meaning. Each of these matters requires only a simple majority for adoption.

Once consideration of both the treaty and the resolution of ratification are completed, and the treaty is reported by the Committee, the treaty is placed on the Executive Calendar. The motion to proceed to the Executive Calendar to consider a treaty is not subject to debate and therefore can easily be resolved by unanimous consent or simple majority vote.

When all debate has ended and there are no additional proposed treaty amendments to consider, the Senate begins consideration of the "resolution of ratification." Once the Senate is considering the resolution of ratification, no further amendments to the treaty itself are in order except by unanimous consent. However, "reservations" to the treaty are only in order during the Senate's consideration of the resolution of ratification. Additional or modified understandings, declarations, statements, or provisos may be added on the Senate floor at this stage of consideration.

Treaties, unlike legislation and nominations, remain before the Senate from Congress to Congress, once submitted by the president. The Genocide Convention was submitted to the Senate by President Harry Truman in 1949. The Senate finally agreed to ratification in 1986.

When the Senate consents to the ratification of a treaty and it is formally ratified by the president, it becomes the supreme law of the land, like the Constitution and federal legislation.

E. The War Powers Resolution

The Framers of the Constitution, consistent with their design of checks and balances, divided the war making powers between the Congress and the president. Article II, Section 2 of the Constitution states that "The President shall be Commander in Chief of the Army and the Navy." However, Article I gives Congress the power "to declare War," and the responsibilities "to raise and support Armies" and "to provide and maintain a Navy."

The shared responsibilities for sending the U.S. military into hostile circumstances have given rise to tensions from time to time between the president and Congress. In the nation's history, Congress has declared war on only five occasions, and not since World War II in 1941. Presidents have submitted more than 120 reports to Congress pursuant to the War Powers Resolution.

To declare war, Congress must pass a joint resolution. This joint resolution is subject to the rules and procedures in both chambers, including the potential for filibuster in the Senate. No senator voted against any of the eleven declarations of war referred to above.

U.S. military forces have been involved in combat situations on numerous occasions without a declaration of war. Public opposition to the war in Vietnam increased substantially from 1963 through 1972, while the war continued under President Richard Nixon from 1969 until U.S. forces were withdrawn from Vietnam in 1975. In response to the growing public opposition, Congress, in 1973, enacted the War Powers Resolution, sometimes referred to as the War Powers Act, over the veto of President Richard Nixon. The War Powers Resolution was intended to establish clear procedures for the president and the Congress to follow in situations that might lead to the involvement of U.S. forces in hostilities abroad.

The War Powers Resolution requires that the president report to Congress, within 48 hours, the use of U.S. armed forces in hostilities or in situations where imminent involvement in hostilities is clearly indicated by the circumstances. Further, the Resolution requires that the president withdraw those forces from hostilities within 60 days, plus an additional 30 days if the president certifies to Congress that the safety of the troops "requires the continued use of such armed forces in the course of bringing about a prompt removal of such forces." The law states that the deadline applies in the absence of "a declaration of war or specific statutory authorization" and can be enforced by the Congress by passage of a joint resolution.

Every president since has maintained that the War Powers Resolution is unconstitutional. They assert it is legislative branch interference with the president's authority as commander in chief. As a result, presidents have submitted numerous reports "consistent with" the law. The implied distinction is that the action is not taken "pursuant to" the War Powers Resolution—acknowledging Congress without conceding constitutional authority.

The extraordinary expedited procedures contained in the War Powers Resolution are designed to facilitate Congress in making a judgment about the authorization of the commitment of the U.S. military. The unusual fast-track procedures can empower any one senator (or member of the House) to force a vote on a joint resolution, restricting the president's ability to commit the armed forces.

F. Congressional Oversight

Congressional oversight plays a fundamental role in the system of checks and balances envisioned by the Constitution. Although not explicitly enumerated, oversight responsibilities are implicit in Congress's constitutional role and have been exercised since the nation's earliest days. Oversight enables Congress to review actions taken by other parts of the federal government.

In *The Federalist* No. 51, James Madison famously wrote:

> "If men were angels, no government would be necessary. If angels governed men, neither external nor internal controls on government would be necessary. In framing a government which is to be administered by men over men, the great difficulty lies in this: you must first enable the government to control the governed; and in the next place, oblige it to control itself."

The Supreme Court has held that Congress's investigatatory power is rooted in the Necessary and Proper Clause of Article I of the Constitution. In a unanimous decision, the Court wrote that "the power of inquiry— with process to enforce it—is an essential and appropriate auxiliary to the legislative function." Congress has routinely examined both the public and private sectors. Overseeing the execution and evaluating the performance of laws passed by Congress by the federal bureaucracy and the private sector is an ever-increasing task. Congressional inquiries have examined not only whether current laws are working, but also whether new laws or tougher agency enforcement actions are needed.

One of the watersheds in congressional oversight was the establishment in 1946 of the Joint Committee on the Organization of Congress, known as the LaFollette-Monroney Committee. That committee, charged with "enabling [Congress] to better meet its responsibilities under the Constitution," shaped the Legislative Reorganization Act of 1946, which was signed into law by President Harry Truman. Truman had pioneered the modernization of congressional oversight as the Chair of the Special Committee to Investigate the National Defense Program, known as the Truman Committee. Then-Senator Truman investigated waste and corruption by contractors and defense agencies during World War II, and his committee is credited with being one of the most effective oversight efforts in congressional history, saving millions of taxpayer dollars.

Among a range of other committee reforms like reducing the number of committees in the Senate from 33 to 15 and in the House from 48 to19, the Legislative Reorganization Act of 1946 directly addressed congressional oversight. Section 136 made the oversight responsibilities of standing congressional committees explicit. The authority granted to each standing committee for this function included the ability to issue subpoenas and to open investigations on matters within their jurisdiction on their own. The practice prior to the 1946 Act had been to create a special committee to investigate individual policy problems as they arose.

Today, both chambers' rules authorize standing committees to conduct oversight investigations. House Rule X provides a general charge of oversight responsibility to the House Committee on Oversight, which is frequently renamed as control of the House shifts. The Committee has been alternatively known as Oversight and Governmental Reform; Oversight and Reform; and Oversight and Accountability. Rule X further mandates "Each standing committee … shall review and study on a continuing basis the application, administration, and execution of all laws within its legislative jurisdiction." In the Senate, Rule XXVI contains virtually the same language regarding standing committees charging them with oversight responsibilities on a "continuing basis."

Another important oversight mechanism available to Congress is the Government Accountability Office (GAO), originally created as the General Accounting Office by the 1921 Budget and Accounting Act. In the years after World War II, GAO's mission shifted from accounting matters to broad investigations and evaluations of federal programs. In recent years, congressional committees, congressional leadership, and individual members of Congress have increasingly sought GAO assistance. As a nonpartisan agency, its audits and reports give added credibility to congressional oversight uncovering inefficiencies, waste, fraud, and wrongdoing. GAO also has jurisdiction to hear and adjudicate bid protests of federal procurements.

Congress also enlists the assistance of the inspectors general (IGs) in the agencies of the federal government. In approximately seventy federal agencies, IGs head permanent, nonpartisan, and independent offices charged with overseeing the efficient and effective operation of those agencies. Established by the Inspector General Act of 1978, IGs are required to report to Congress every six months on their activities. They are unique in the executive branch in that they report directly to Congress as well as to the head of their home agency. Their findings and reports are not reviewed by or filtered through their agency, an important element of their ability to be independent. In the event of discovery of egregious abuses within a federal agency, the IG is required to immediately notify the agency head and then the Congress within seven days. Cabinet-level departments and some other large agencies have IGs who are appointed by the president with the advice and consent of the Senate. The Inspector General Act includes among its principal purposes "keeping... the Congress fully and currently informed about problems and deficiencies relating to the administration of ... programs and operations and the necessity for and progress of corrective action."

Committees also wield powerful legal tools in conducting oversight or investigations, including subpoena powers, deposition authority, grants of congressional immunity (sometimes used to gain testimony of witnesses who have asserted their Fifth Amendment rights not to incriminate themselves), and the potential to hold witnesses in contempt of Congress for failing to provide requested information. Whether provided through public testimony under oath or statements made in more private settings, and whether sworn or unsworn, federal law prohibits making false statements to Congress.

Some committees have left a lasting mark on oversight practice. The Senate Permanent Subcommittee on Investigations (PSI) within the Homeland Security and Governmental Affairs Committee, a descendant of the Truman Committee, was notoriously used by Senator Joseph McCarthy in the 1950s to investigate alleged Communist infiltration of the U.S. government. When his closed sessions were made public after fifty years and showed Senator McCarthy berating and badgering witnesses, then-Chair Carl Levin and Ranking Member Susan Collins wrote that "These hearings are a part of our national past that we can neither afford to forget nor permit to reoccur." Because the Subcommittee, or PSI as it is known, did not forget, it has distinguished itself by meeting high standards for conducting fact-based, bipartisan, professional oversight on a broad range of issues, such as money laundering, Oil-for Food at the United Nations, offshore tax abuses, unfair credit card practices, health care fraud, aviation disasters, and egregious tax avoidance.

Oversight of the intelligence community of the United States raises special issues because of the secrecy and national security demands that must be weighed against transparency and accountability norms in an open and democratic system. To address those issues, the Senate created the Select Committee on Intelligence (SSCI) in 1976 and the House created the Permanent Select Committee on Intelligence (HPSCI) in 1977. The committees grew out of recommendations made by the Senate's "Church Committee" (formally the Senate Select Committee to Study Governmental Operations with Respect to Intelligence Activities), which published its final report in April 1976, and the House's Pike Committee that was chaired by Representative Otis Pike. The select intelligence committees do not have exclusive jurisdiction over issues involving the intelligence community; oversight can also be exercised in both chambers by the Armed Services Committees, the Appropriations Committee, the Foreign Relations Committee (Foreign Affairs in the House), and the Judiciary Committees.

Committees with broad, overlapping jurisdictions are common in Congress. In the intelligence context, since many of the intelligence committee hearings and analyses are shielded from the public, attendance and involvement in the work of the select committee by members other than the chair and vice chair has been a fairly consistent problem, making the ability of other committees to examine intelligence issues an ongoing benefit.

G. Investigations

Congressional oversight can take many forms, with various levels of intensity. The most intense form of congressional oversight is conducting a lengthy and detailed investigation.

Investigations share many characteristics with general oversight functions, although they tend to be more adversarial. The ultimate goal is to improve Congress's ability to carry out its legislative role in addressing matters of public policy in both the private and public sectors by assessing the executive branch's implementation of current laws, exposing private sector abuses, and determining whether new laws are needed.

Because witnesses in an investigatory context may be less forthcoming, they may be subjected to subpoenas compelling them to provide documents or testimony, brought in for lengthy interviews, placed under oath, or perhaps brought before the committee in a public hearing. Witnesses subject to committee inquiries, of course, retain Constitutional rights, including the Fifth Amendment protection against self-incrimination.

Congressional investigations can capture significant attention, both in the process of convening public hearings and in releasing long-form written reports. Even for classified subjects, unclassified reports can reach wide audiences. For example, in late 2014 the Senate Select Committee on Intelligence released a 500-page unclassified synopsis of its report into the investigation of the Central Intelligence Agency's interrogation and detention programs. That report and the surrounding investigation were even dramatized in a 2019 movie.

In the late 1980s, House and Senate select committees held a series of joint hearings to investigate a series of intertwined scandals known colloquially as Iran-Contra. Retrospective analysis of the Iran-Contra hearings have underscored the importance of comprehensive, bicameral, and bipartisan oversight, and explored the challenges associated with publicizing a process that, despite having some trappings of legal procedure, is fundamentally a political exercise.

H. Congressional Review Act

Given the complexity of implementing many laws and regulations, Congress regularly delegates rulemaking authority to the president, to the executive branch, and to independent agencies. Congress can oversee this authority through oversight and appropriations work. A more powerful tool is the Congressional Review Act, passed in 1996, which provides a period of time for Congress to consider and overturn a rule issued by a federal agency before it takes effect. This provision can be especially significant following a presidential election when the presidency changes hands.

Under the Congressional Review Act, agencies submit a report to Congress laying out the details of a new rule. Any member of the House or Senate may introduce a joint resolution of disapproval of any final agency rule. Congress then considers the joint resolution to disapprove the rule under expedited procedures that provide for a 60-day window in which the Congress may act, and that limits debate on that joint resolution, thus eliminating the possibility of a filibuster in the Senate. This means that only a simple majority is needed in both chambers to pass a joint resolution of disapproval.

If both the House and the Senate pass a resolution of disapproval, it may be signed or vetoed by the president. If a resolution of disapproval is enacted by Congress and signed by the president, or in the rare event that a presidential veto of the resolution is overridden, the rule is voided and cannot be reemployed in "substantially the same form" unless Congress has enacted a new law authorizing the rule. If a rule is submitted late enough that the 60-day window for action under the Congressional Review Act does not expire prior to *sine die* adjournment, a new period of review opens for the new Congress.

I. Impeachment

Article I, Section 2 of the Constitution grants to the House the authority to impeach the president, other executive branch officials, and federal judges and justices. Article II, Section 4 states: "The President, Vice President and all civil Officers of the United States, shall be removed from Office on Impeachment for, and Conviction of, Treason, Bribery, or other high Crimes and Misdemeanors." Much debate has focused on the words "high crimes and misdemeanors," since its meaning in a legal context is not clear. Impeachment and trial in Congress is principally a political process, not a legal one.

Impeachment in the House is similar to indictment. Impeachment requires a simple majority vote in the House, a quorum having been established. Impeachment may be initiated by any member of the House of Representatives by submitting a House resolution. The resolution is referred to the House Judiciary Committee. Individual "articles of impeachment" are voted on and reported by the Judiciary Committee, and then by the full House.

The Senate, under Article I, Section 3, possesses the "sole Power to try all Impeachments." It is the Senate that determines whether to convict and remove from office any impeached official. House managers are appointed to argue the case before the Senate. Conviction requires a two-thirds vote of senators present. When the president is tried, the Chief Justice of the United States presides in the Senate trial. The vice president or President *pro tempore* presides over other impeachment trials.

Since the nation's founding, the House has impeached 21 individuals, including six since 1986 (prior to 1986, there had not been an impeachment for 50 years). Only eight officials, all federal judges, have been convicted by the Senate in its history. Only one Supreme Court justice has been impeached, Samuel Chase in 1804. Chase was accused by the Jeffersonian Republican-controlled House of allowing his Federalist proclivities to infect judicial proceedings, particularly ones involving politically charged matters. He was acquitted by the Senate on all eight articles of impeachment, because none of the articles garnered the two-thirds majority vote necessary to convict and remove him.

The House has impeached three presidents: Andrew Johnson in 1868, over his firing of Secretary of War Edwin Stanton; Bill Clinton in 1998, over alleged perjury before a grand jury and obstruction of justice; and Donald Trump twice, in 2019 and 2021, for abuse of power and obstruction of Congress, and for incitement of insurrection in connection with the January 6, 2021 attack on the U.S. Capitol. All three presidents were acquitted by the Senate.

President Andrew Johnson came closest to removal. The Senate voted 35-19 to remove him, one vote short of the necessary two-thirds (there were only 54 senators at the time). President Clinton was acquitted on both articles of impeachment with 55 votes for acquittal and 45 for conviction on the perjury charge, and 50 votes for acquittal and 50 votes for conviction on the obstruction of justice charge. President Trump was acquitted with 52 votes for acquittal on the abuse charge and 53 votes on the obstruction charge in 2020, and with 43 votes for acquittal on the single charge in 2021.

President Richard Nixon was seriously threatened with impeachment during the Watergate scandal. The House vote to give formal authority to the Judiciary Committee to consider impeachment of Nixon passed 410-4. In July 1974, the House Judiciary Committee reported three articles of impeachment against Nixon—obstruction of justice, abuse of power, and contempt of Congress—by a bipartisan majority. Seven of the Committee's 17 Republicans voted for the abuse of power article. Two additional articles were proposed, but defeated.

On August 8, 1974, a small group of members headed by Senator Barry Goldwater went to the White House to warn the president that if he did not resign from office, the House would impeach him and the Senate would likely remove him from office. The next day, August 9, 1974, Nixon resigned before the House could impeach him. His successor, President Gerald Ford, pardoned Nixon for any wrongdoing he may have committed.

J. Twenty-Fifth Amendment

The Twenty-Fifth Amendment, ratified in 1967 in the wake of President Kennedy's assassination, clarified procedures for the replacement of a president or vice president upon death, disability, or removal from office.

The amendment was invoked several times during the Watergate era in the 1970s. In 1973, Vice President Spiro Agnew resigned in the face of corruption and tax evasion charges, and Congressman Gerald Ford was named and confirmed to replace him. Less than a year later, in August 1974, when Richard Nixon resigned the presidency, Ford became president and named Nelson Rockefeller to fill the vacant vice presidency. When a nominee is chosen by the president to assume the office of vice president, that appointment must be confirmed by a majority vote of both the House of Representatives and the Senate.

Congress also plays a critical role should the vice president and a majority of the cabinet, acting under Section 4 of the Twenty-Fifth Amendment, declare the president unable to discharge the powers and duties of the office. If the president resists that declaration by asserting the capacity to discharge those powers and duties, the president would resume authority unless, by a two-thirds vote of each chamber, Congress determines otherwise.

While Congress has always had the power to remove a president through impeachment and conviction, the Twenty-Fifth Amendment is meant to provide a way for the vice president, the cabinet, and Congress to remove a president temporarily or permanently under dire circumstances when the president is ill or otherwise incapacitated. Section 4 has never been invoked.

K. Recess and Adjournment

An adjournment motion is the formal action to end the daily session of either the House or Senate. The adjournment motion may establish the day or time that the House or Senate will next convene. When the Senate or House adjourns for the final time, it adjourns *sine die*.

By contrast, a recess in the Senate or House is generally a temporary interruption of business, occurring on occasion within the same day. The Senate also at times recesses rather than adjourning at the end of the day.

Somewhat confusingly, the term "recess" is used to refer to periods in which the House or Senate is adjourned pursuant to a concurrent resolution within sessions of Congress. Such periods within a congressional session are formally known as an "intrasession recess," but colloquially as a "district work period" or "state work period." The Speaker is authorized to declare recesses in the House. Often recesses are declared in the House "at the call of the chair."

In the Senate, the distinction between recessing at the end of the day and adjourning is very significant. Whether the Senate recesses or adjourns at the end of the day determines, for example, "legislative days" and "calendar days." A calendar day for the purposes of the Senate is understood to be a 24-hour period. However, a legislative day ends when the Senate adjourns.

The Senate majority leader sometimes chooses to recess in order to avoid triggering a number of burdensome requirements that the Senate Rules (Rules V, VII, and XIV) require at the outset of a new legislative day. When the majority leader wishes the Senate to adjourn, they typically seeks unanimous consent to waive these requirements for the next legislative day. If the majority leader is unable to obtain the necessary unanimous consent, recess becomes the easier option. A legislative day may therefore continue for days or weeks.

Majority Leader Robert Byrd made it a frequent practice to recess rather than adjourn. In 1980, he kept the Senate in one long legislative day from January 3 to June 12 by repeatedly recessing. After a two-second adjournment on June 12, the Senate moved on to the next legislative day.

The two chambers may use recess to gain leverage over each other. The Constitution provides that "Neither House, during the session of Congress, shall, without the consent of the other, adjourn for more than three days…" One example already mentioned is the use of this Constitutional requirement by the House—if controlled by the opposition party—to deny permission for the Senate to recess or adjourn for more than three days. This prevents recess appointments by the president. There are also times when one chamber or the other threatens to adjourn in order to leave the other chamber with a "take-it-or-leave-it" proposition on passing a particular version of a bill.

L. Senate Morning Business

Upon reconvening, a new legislative day in the Senate begins, triggering a number of procedural requirements. The first two hours at the outset of a new legislative day are called the morning hour.

The term morning hour is often confused, even by some senators, with "morning business." Morning business is a period *within* the morning hour intended to be used to conduct a number of routine tasks, such as introducing bills and resolutions, receiving presidential messages and messages from the House, filing committee reports, and other actions.

To keep the Senate operating smoothly and to avoid time-consuming routine actions at the outset of each new legislative day, the majority leader or a designee will seek unanimous consent at some earlier time to dispose of some of the requirements and to move others to a more convenient time. For example, the majority leader may say:

> I ask unanimous consent that when the Senate completes its business today, it adjourn until the hour of 10 a.m. on Friday, [date]. I further ask unanimous consent that on Friday, immediately following the prayer, the Journal of proceedings be approved to date, the morning hour be deemed expired, the time for the two leaders be reserved for their use later in the day, and the Senate then begin a period for morning business, with Senators permitted to speak for up to 5 minutes each.

Such unanimous consent agreements have become a common part of each session. The resultant period of morning business is a block of time during the Senate day when senators may go to the floor and speak briefly on any matter they choose. Sometimes unanimous consent allows a senator to consume a longer block of time in morning business. In recent years, both parties have on occasion organized members of their caucus to come to the floor together or in sequence to speak on a particular subject they want to highlight. Therefore, while morning business has become a common term in Senate parlance, the term "morning hour" is more arcane.

M. House Special Orders

Somewhat like morning business speeches in the Senate, members of the House are usually able to make speeches—known as "special orders"—at the end of the day, after the House has completed all legislative business. Members reserve special orders in advance through their party's leadership. Because the House Rules limit debate in both the House of Representatives and the Committee of the Whole House, special orders play an even more important role in that chamber than do morning business speeches in the Senate. Special orders provide a rare opportunity for House members to speak on non-germane subjects and sometimes at length, with a 60-minute limit. Most special order speeches are less than five minutes.

Both morning business in the Senate and special orders in the House have gained importance since the onset of television coverage by C-SPAN. Television coverage of the House began in 1979 and of the Senate in 1986. House Rules place broadcast coverage of proceedings under the exclusive control of the Speaker.

Both chambers prohibit cameras from panning the floor, to avoid showing the chambers empty or senators or House members appearing inattentive. This prohibition was temporarily suspended for a few days in early 2023, during a contested and drawn-out process to elect a new Speaker. During the hours and days of voting that eventually led to Kevin McCarthy's election, the House had no Speaker, and thus no formal rules in place, including the rule that normally prohibits camera panning. As a result, the cameras lingered on members and groups, and captured multiple minor dramas as they played out across the House floor, including one episode when a senior member appeared to be physically restrained from assaulting a colleague.

N. Rulings and Appeals of Rulings of the Chair

Senate Rule XX states that a "question of order may be raised at any stage of the proceedings, except when the Senate is voting or ascertaining the presence of a quorum, and, unless submitted to the Senate, shall be decided by the Presiding Officer without debate, subject to an appeal to the Senate." Rulings on these matters follow the advice of the Senate parliamentarian, a professional, non-partisan official.

An important feature of the Senate is that when the presiding officer rules on a point of order—or when an appeal of that ruling is successful—a new precedent is established. These precedents have the full force and effect of a Senate rule.

O. Expelling a Member or Denying a Seat to a Member-Elect

Article I, Section 5 of the Constitution states: "Each House shall be the Judge of the Elections, Returns and Qualifications of its own Members." Under this provision, the Senate may decline to seat a senator-elect and the House may refuse to seat a representative-elect by a simple majority vote.

This step may be taken if the chamber finds that the member-elect fails to meet the qualifications for office in that body set out in the Constitution. This Constitutional right to exclude a member-elect was circumscribed by the Supreme Court in a 1969 case. In 1967, the House voted 307 to 116 to exclude Congressman Adam Clayton Powell (D-NY) from being re-seated in the 90th Congress. The House found that Powell had engaged in deceptive and possibly illegal actions surrounding his prior service as chair of the House Committee on Education and Labor in a preceding Congress. The 7–1 decision in *Powell v. McCormack* held that the House could not exclude a duly elected member unless he failed to meet the Constitutional requirements of age, citizenship, or residence: "Congress is limited to the standing qualifications described in the Constitution."

Article I, Section 5 also states: "Each House may... punish its Members for disorderly Behavior, and, with the Concurrence of two thirds, expel a Member." Each chamber may execute these disciplinary powers without the concurrence of the other chamber and has wide authority regarding the grounds and procedure for expelling a member. Other punishments short of expulsion are available, including censure, reprimand, and removal from committee assignments.

The constitutional grounds for expulsion are much broader than those for exclusion. A chamber may choose whatever grounds it deems appropriate to expel a member, as long as it musters a two-thirds vote. For example, the House may expel a member for "conduct reflecting discredit on the House."

Although the power to expel is robust, it has been employed sparingly. Lesser punishments have been more common.

Since 1789 the Senate has censured nine senators, the most prominent being Joseph McCarthy in 1954. The most recent censures were Thomas J. Dodd in 1967, Herman E. Talmadge in 1979, and David F. Durenberger in 1990. As of March 2025, twenty-eight members of the House have been censured (including three members in 2023 alone) and another eleven reprimanded.

The Senate in its history has only expelled fifteen senators. Fourteen of those were for treason or supporting the rebellion during the Civil War. No senator has been expelled since 1862. Only five members of the House have been expelled, the first three for disloyalty during the Civil War. More recently, Congressman Michael Myers was expelled in 1980 after conviction for bribery in the FBI's sting operation known as ABSCAM. In 2002, Congressman James Traficant was expelled after conviction for bribery and obstruction of justice. In 2023, Congressman George Santos was expelled after he "knowingly caused his campaign committee to file false or incomplete reports with the Federal Election Commission, used campaign funds for personal purposes, engaged in fraudulent conduct ... and engaged in knowing and willful violations of the Ethics in Government Act."

In more recent times, when the likelihood of expulsion seemed imminent, senators have resigned rather than suffer expulsion. Senator Bob Packwood was accused of sexual harassment by twenty women, and resigned when it became clear that his expulsion was certain. Senator Harrison Williams, also caught in the FBI's ABSCAM sting operation, was convicted of bribery and conspiracy. He was the first senator convicted of a crime since 1906. He did not resign until eight days after the floor debate in the Senate had begun on the resolution to expel him. When expulsion seemed a certainty, he stepped down. Senator Robert Menendez, a former chairman of the Foreign Relations Committee, resigned in 2024, a month after his conviction on federal bribery charges.

An issue widely discussed with respect to this case is whether the Senate and its Ethics Committee would have jurisdiction over an incident that occurred before a member took office. This question arose in 2007 in the case of Senator David Vitter who admitted to having committed a "very serious sin" after his solicitation of prostitutes came to light. The occurrences happened prior to the senator's election to the Senate. The Senate Ethics Committee dismissed the case on the grounds that the behavior had occurred prior to Vitter's election, and did not involve criminal charges or involve improper use of his public office. The Committee did state, however, that "…based upon these specific grounds, the committee has determined that it should *not further exercise its jurisdiction over this matter at this time*." [emphasis added] This appears to at least leave open the question of whether the Vitter precedent would preclude future Ethics Committee investigations into cases in which the alleged offense occurred prior to election.

The powers of exclusion and expulsion given to each chamber are the only ways that a representative or a senator may be removed from or denied office. There is no provision for recall of federal elected officials by their electorate or by state legislatures. Even the judiciary is not given the Constitutional power to remove a member of Congress.

P. Presidential Election

Congress plays an important role in the quadrennial election of the president and vice president. Article II, Section 1 of the Constitution, as modified by the Twelfth Amendment, establishes Congress's role in the Electoral College system. Under these constitutional provisions and federal law, Congress meets in joint session on January 6 (a date fixed by statute) following a presidential election to receive and count electoral ballots, and the election of the president and vice president is announced formally by the outgoing vice president (as president of the Senate). Congress is also empowered to resolve objections regarding those ballots.

To be elected president or vice president by the Electoral College, a candidate must receive a majority, and not merely a plurality, of the electoral ballots (currently 270 of 538). The Twelfth Amendment, as modified by the 20th Amendment, outlines the procedures to be followed in the event that no candidate for president or vice president attains a majority of the electoral ballots. In the case of the president, the House of Representatives chooses the president from among the three candidates with the largest numbers of electoral ballots; each state delegation casts a single vote. A majority of states is needed for election. In the case of the vice presidential candidate, the Senate must choose between the two candidates with the largest number of electoral ballots. Each senator has one vote, and a majority of votes is needed for election.

These divergent provisions could produce strange outcomes. For example, for much of the spring and summer of 1992 in the presidential election campaign, polls showed incumbent President George H.W. Bush and Independent challenger Ross Perot trading the lead. Democrat Bill Clinton was polling a distant third. If those placements held on election day, and no candidate received a majority of electoral votes, the presidential election would have been determined in the House of Representatives. Even if the Democratic House had elected Clinton, his running mate Al Gore would not have been an eligible candidate for vice president, since he would have been the third-place finisher. The Senate's only options in the top two would be incumbent Vice President Dan Quayle or Perot's running mate, retired Admiral James Stockdale.

Q. Electoral Count Reform Act

The 2020 election brought national attention to Congress's role in the transfer of presidential power. The attack on the Capitol on January 6, 2021, marked the culmination of weeks in which allies of President Trump raised doubts about the validity of states' elections, and argued for radical interpretations of provisions of the Constitution and the Electoral Count Act that, in their view, would allow the vice president to nullify slates of electoral votes.

In the aftermath, Congress revised the Electoral Count Act. In 2022, Congress passed—and President Biden signed—the Electoral Count Reform and Presidential Transition Improvement Act ("ECRA"). ECRA amended several procedures governing state election conduct and certification of electoral votes, and clarified the jurisdiction of federal courts to adjudicate disputes efficiently.

ECRA also made two key changes that affect Congress's role in convening and counting votes. First, it strictly limited the role for the vice president, as president of the Senate, in the counting process: "the role of the President of the Senate while presiding over the joint session shall be limited to performing solely ministerial duties. The President of the Senate shall have no power to solely determine, accept, reject, or otherwise adjudicate or resolve disputes over the proper certificate of ascertainment of appointment of electors, the validity of electors, or the votes of electors."

Second, it raised the threshold for objections. Whereas the original Electoral Count Act permitted a single member and single Senator to object to a state's electoral votes, ECRA now requires one-fifth of both chambers to sign on to objections. ECRA also limits the grounds for objections to two: either that "electors of the State were not lawfully certified under a certificate of ascertainment of appointment of electors" or that "[t]he vote of one or more electors has not been regularly given." Reasonable people may disagree whether those latter provisions, had they been in effect on January 6, 2021, would have impeded the effort to undermine the 2020 election results, given the initially significant amount of Republican support for the challenges. But they now raise the stakes for members and senators who must make the initial move to challenge a state's electoral votes.

R. Presidential Succession

Article II, Section 1 of the Constitution, as modified by the Twenty-Fifth Amendment, specifies that the "Vice President shall become President" upon the president's death, resignation, or removal from office. This has occurred eight times in American history. It is left to Congress, however, to determine the order of succession to the presidency should both the president and vice president be dead or removed from office.

The Twenty-Fifth Amendment also provides a process for filling a vacancy in the vice presidency. Before its ratification, although seven vice presidents had died in office and one had resigned, there was no mechanism for filling the office. The nation had been fortunate that although it has been without a vice president in office for a combined total of nearly 38 years, no president died or resigned during those periods. The assassination of President Kennedy in 1963 left Lyndon Johnson without a vice president for more than a year, spurring Congress to act. The Twenty-Fifth Amendment was passed in 1965 and ratified by the states in 1967. It also establishes procedures for handling presidential incapacitation.

The current Presidential Succession Act, 3 U.S.C. § 19, provides that the Speaker of the House of Representatives, the President *pro tempore* of the Senate, and duly-confirmed cabinet officers, in order of the creation of their departments, would be eligible to act as president. This is the third iteration of succession laws. The first was passed by the Second Congress, the Succession Act of 1792, which provided for the President *pro tempore* of the Senate and the Speaker of the House of Representatives, in that order, to assume the presidency. This first succession law also provided for a special election for the presidency. No such special election has ever occurred.

The second, enacted in 1886 after the death of President James Garfield during a period when there was neither a President *pro tempore* nor a Speaker of the House in place, removed the Congressional Constitutional officers and placed cabinet officers in the line of succession after the vice president.

The current law, the Presidential Succession Act of 1947, returned the Constitutional officers to the line of succession but reversed their order. The Speaker of the House of Representatives is first, then the President *pro tempore*, followed by cabinet officers beginning with the Secretary of State. A little-noticed provision, called "bumping rights," provides that if a cabinet officer is serving as acting president, that individual can be replaced at any time by the Speaker or the President *pro tempore*.

S. Congress and the Courts

The Constitution created the Supreme Court but left it to Congress to establish by law whatever additional lower courts it deemed necessary. Article III, Section 1 states: "The judicial Power of the United States, shall be vested in one supreme Court, and in such inferior Courts as the Congress may from time to time ordain and establish."

Congress determines the Supreme Court's budget, the salaries of justices, and aspects of its jurisdiction, to the extent consistent with the Constitution. Congress also determines these factors for lower courts that it has created, including the federal district courts and the circuit courts of appeal. The president appoints federal judges and justices for life terms, with the advice and consent of the Senate, and subject to removal only through impeachment.

The Constitution allows Congress to decide how many justices sit on the Supreme Court. Currently, the Court has nine justices. Originally, the

Judiciary Act of 1789 set the number of justices at six. Eighteen years later, it was raised to seven. The number first reached nine in 1837 and rose to ten in 1863, its largest size in U.S. history. Since 1869, the Court has remained at nine justices, aside from occasional vacancies.

The most serious challenge to this arrangement came in 1937, when President Franklin Roosevelt proposed to Congress a court reform bill that would have enlarged the Supreme Court to as many as fifteen justices. Thought to be motivated by FDR's desire for a court more friendly to his New Deal legislation, the plan came to be known as "court packing," and was roundly rejected by the Senate, 70–22.

T. Amending the Constitution

Article V of the Constitution gives Congress a central role in amending the nation's foundational document: "The Congress, whenever two thirds of both Houses shall deem it necessary, shall propose Amendments to this Constitution…which…shall be valid to all Intents and Purposes, as Part of this Constitution, when ratified by the Legislatures of three fourths of the several States…." An alternative method of conventions called by the states is also included in Article V, but has never been used. The president has no constitutional role in the amendment process.

Constitutional amendments may be proposed by any member of Congress in the form of a joint resolution, although unlike other joint resolutions, they do not require the president's signature to take effect. A joint resolution may be introduced in the House (H.J. Res.) or Senate (S.J. Res.). Joint resolutions proposing to amend the Constitution are referred to the House and Senate Judiciary Committees.

If reported by the committee to either the House or the Senate, they are considered under ordinary legislative rules. In the Senate, they are subject to amendment and in the House they may also be amended consistent with House rules.

The Constitution requires a vote of two-thirds of members of each house, present and voting, a quorum being present. Should the House and Senate pass differing versions of the amendment, a conference committee would be needed. Adoption of the conference report would require another two-thirds vote in each chamber.

Since 1789, the Constitution has been amended 27 times, including by the Bill of Rights, the first ten amendments, that were ratified together in 1791. Seven amendments adopted by Congress and transmitted to the states have failed. Beginning with the Eighteenth Amendment (Prohibition), with one exception (the repeal of Prohibition), Congress has usually included a time limit for ratification in its joint resolutions proposing Constitutional amendments. Without such a provision, there is no limit to the time elapsed before a sufficient number of states might ratify an amendment. The most recent amendment, the Twenty-Seventh, took more than 202 years. Originally proposed in 1789 by James Madison for inclusion in the Bill of Rights, it required that any change in congressional pay take effect only after the next election. It was adopted in 1789 by the First Congress but was not ratified by the requisite number of states until Michigan ratified it in 1992.

The Equal Rights Amendment (ERA) illustrates the complexity of the process. Congress passed the ERA in 1972 with a seven-year time limit, later extended to 1982. At the deadline only 35 states had ratified, three short of the required 38 (three-fourths of states). By 2020, 38 states had ratified the amendment, but others had purported to "rescind" their ratification after changes in political control, casting doubt on the continued validity of the states' original ratification. Whether a rescission has legal effect, and whether Congress can constitutionally enforce a deadline on ratification, remain unresolved questions.

The process laid out in Article V has never changed. All amendments to the Constitution that have been adopted have been proposed by Congress. All but the Twenty-First Amendment, which repealed the Eighteenth Amendment (Prohibition), were ratified by state legislatures. The Twenty-First Amendment was ratified in 1933 by the vote of state conventions of three-fourths of the states.

Chapter 10
Conclusion

The Founders intended to place Congress at the heart of our national government. Much of this book has focused on and attempted to explain what is commonly called the "regular order," the normal legislative procedures established by the rules and precedents.

Yet the process of lawmaking has been repeatedly disrupted by cycles of procedural hardball, with the majority pressing its advantages and the minority responding with obstruction and delay. Both major political parties have taken their turn, and the cumulative effect has been an erosion of courtesy, comity, and deliberation.

Our politics have become more polarized, political parties have become more closely aligned with ideological beliefs, congressional leadership has centralized, and the parties have moved farther and farther apart.

Whatever the origins, many now believe Congress is more polarized than at any time since at least Reconstruction and the Civil War. This cannot be healthy for a democracy.

This hyper-partisan polarization has set up a repeating cycle of action and reaction in the legislative branch. Procedure, tradition, and precedent are used for short-term partisan gain, and the victim party strikes back with whatever procedural tool is at hand.

The sources of political information—increasingly unreliable and subject to intentional manipulation by malicious actors—intensify this process, amplifying partisan combat and demanding shortcuts in the legislative process.

This book discusses in detail many of these practices that, even though they fall outside of the regular order and distort the rules and precedents, have come to dominate the proceedings of Congress. Recognizing them is crucial to understanding why Congress is struggling to function as intended, and to building and executing effective legislative strategies under the conditions as they exist.

Recent years have seen a sharp increase in the use of the filibuster by minorities in the Senate, the use of the nuclear option to advantage the majority, the exploitation of the 30 hours permitted post-cloture to frustrate the majority's agenda, holds to slow progress in the Senate, reconciliation beyond its original scope, filling the amendment tree by majority leaders in the Senate to block minority amendments, closed rules in the House, fewer conference committees, greater use of informal negotiations, and the near collapse of a timely appropriations process.

We have repeatedly seen a preference for expediency in the service of partisan advantage, exacerbated by a decline in civility and the near-constant vilification of the opposition.

The Founders, in Article I, Section 5, empowered Congress to write its own rules. This was a fundamental protection of the independence of the legislative branch in the system of checks and balances. Those rules and the procedures they frame, the regular order of the Congress, continue to protect that independence and are crucial to the stability and resilience of the House and Senate in their protection of American freedoms and the rule of law.

Democracy is something more than majority rule. It also involves protection of the rights of the minority. Our democratic process operates on the assumption that both parties will act in good faith, and protect the norms and interests inherent in the constitutional framework. Congress must have the flexibility and courage to negotiate, moderate, and compromise. In other words, to legislate.

Glossary

Act: Legislation that has passed both houses of Congress and been signed by the president, or passed over a veto, thus becoming law. Also, a parliamentary term for a measure that has been passed by one chamber and engrossed.

Adjourn: Formal motion to end a day's session of a chamber of Congress.

Adjourn *Sine Die*: Final adjournment of a session of Congress.

Adoption (Adopted): Usual parliamentary term for approval of a conference report.

Advice and Consent: Constitutional role (Article II, Section 2) given to the Senate to confirm nominations (executive branch and judicial) by simple majority, and treaties by a two-thirds vote.

Agreed To: Usual parliamentary term for approval of motions, amendments, and simple and concurrent resolutions.

Amendment: Proposal of a member of Congress to alter the text of a measure.

Amendment in the Nature of a Substitute: Amendment that seeks to replace the entire text of the underlying measure. The adoption of such an amendment usually precludes any further amendment to that measure.

Amendment Tree: Diagram showing the number and types of amendments to a measure permitted by the chamber. It also shows the relationship among the amendments, their degree or type, and the order in which they may be offered and voted on.

Amendment Tree (Filling of): Procedure used by the Senate majority leader to offer enough amendments to preclude other senators from offering amendments. This tactic is sometimes used to exclude amendments by the minority.

Amendments Between the Houses: Method for reconciling differences between the two chambers' versions of a measure by passing the measure back and forth until both have agreed to identical language. Colloquially known as the "ping pong" approach to reconciling differences in legislation. *Contrast with* Conference Committee.

Appeal: A member's challenge to a ruling made by the presiding officer or a committee chair. In the Senate, on a point of order, any senator may appeal a ruling of the presiding officer.

Appropriation: Provision of law providing budget authority that permits federal agencies to incur obligations and make payments out of the Treasury. *See also* Budget Authority.

Appropriations Bill: Bill that, if enacted as law, gives legal authority to spend or obligate money from the Treasury. *See also* Budget Authority.

Authorization: Provision in law that establishes or continues a program or agency and authorizes appropriations for it.

Baseline: Projection of future revenues, budget authority, outlays, and other budget amounts under assumed economic conditions and participation rates without a change in current policy.

Bigger Bite: An amendment that can be offered because it changes more of the measure or amendment than the original amendment, notwithstanding the general prohibition on amending previously amended language.

Bill: Measure that becomes law when passed in identical form by both chambers and signed by the president or passed over a veto. Designated as *H.R.* or *S. See also* Joint Resolution.

Blue-Slip Resolution: House resolution ordering the return to the Senate of a Senate bill or amendment that the House believes violates the constitutional prerogative of the House to originate revenue measures.

Blue-Slip (Senate): Informal process imposed by chairs of the Senate Judiciary Committee to assess the approval or disapproval by home-state senators of appointees from their states.

Borrowing Authority: Spending authority that permits a federal agency to incur obligations and make payments for specified purposes out of funds borrowed from the Treasury or the public.

Budget Authority: Authority in law to enter into obligations that normally result in outlays.

Budget Resolution: Concurrent resolution incorporating an agreement by the House and Senate on an overall budget plan; may contain reconciliation instructions.

By Request: A designation on a measure that appears next to the sponsor's name and indicates that a member has introduced the measure on behalf of the president, an executive agency, or a private individual or organization.

Byrd Rule: Bars the inclusion of extraneous matter in a reconciliation measure considered in the Senate.

Chairman's Mark: Early draft of a bill reflecting recommendations by committee (or subcommittee) leaders of the measure to be considered in a markup.

Christmas Tree: Jargon for a bill containing many amendments unrelated to the bill's main subject.

Cloture: Process by which a filibuster can be ended in the Senate.

Colloquy: Discussion between members during floor proceedings, generally to put on the record a mutual understanding about the intent of a provision or amendment. The discussion is usually scripted in advance.

Committee of the Whole: The House in a different parliamentary form. It is a committee consisting of all members of the House, where measures are considered for amendment. The quorum is one hundred. Members are generally permitted to speak for five minutes. A chair presides in lieu of the Speaker.

Committee Report: Document accompanying a measure reported from a committee. It contains an explanation of the provisions of the measure, arguments for its approval, and other information.

Companion Bills: Identical or similar bills introduced in both chambers.

Concur: Agree to an amendment of the other chamber, either as offered or with a further amendment.

Concurrent Resolution: A measure adopted by both the House and Senate, designated as *H. Con. Res.* or *S. Con. Res.*, that does not require presidential approval or have the force of law. It takes effect only if passed in identical form by both houses and is used to express the sentiment of Congress or to carry out the administrative business of both chambers.

Conferees: Representatives from each chamber who serve on a conference committee.

Conference Committee: Temporary joint committee created to resolve differences between the chambers on a measure. *Contrast with* Amendment Between the Houses.

Conference Report: Document containing a conference committee's agreements and signed by a majority of conferees from each chamber. *See also* Joint Explanatory Statement of Managers.

Continuing Appropriations Act: A stop-gap appropriations measure, also referred to as a continuing resolution (CR), that provides temporary funding for federal agencies when regular appropriations bills have not been enacted.

Cordon Rule: Senate rule that requires a committee report to show how a reported measure would change current law. *See also* Ramseyer Rule.

Cost Estimate: An estimate of the impact of legislation on revenues, spending, or both, generally as reported by a House or Senate committee or a conference committee. Under the 1974 Congressional Budget Act, the Congressional Budget Office must prepare cost estimates for all public bills.

Custody of the Papers: Custody of the engrossed measure and related documents that the two chambers produce as they try to reconcile differences in their versions of a measure. *See* Papers.

Deferral: Action or inaction that temporarily withholds, delays, or effectively precludes the obligation or expenditure of budget authority.

Deficit: Excess of outlays over revenues.

Degrees of Amendment: Designations showing the relationship of an amendment to the text of a measure and to other amendments. Only two degrees are permitted. *See* Amendment Tree.

Direct Spending: Spending controlled outside of annual appropriations acts; also called mandatory spending. *See also* Entitlement Program; *contrast with* Discretionary Spending.

Disagree: To reject an amendment adopted by the other chamber.

Discharge Calendar: House calendar listing motions to discharge committees which have received 218 signatures.

Discharge Petition: Procedure to remove a measure from committee and make it available for floor consideration, regardless of the Speaker's or Rules Committee's preference.

Discretionary Spending: Spending provided in, and controlled by, annual appropriations acts. *Contrast with* Direct Spending.

Division Vote: A vote in which the committee chair or House presiding officer counts those members in favor and those in opposition to a proposition with no record made of how each voted. The chair can either ask for a show of hands or ask members to stand.

Earmark: For expenditures, an amount set aside within an appropriations account for a specified purpose, sometimes called "Member-directed spending." The term is also used for targeted tax provisions benefitting an individual, small group, or specific corporation, as well as for specific projects or programs included in the President's budget request.

Electronic Vote: A vote in the House using electronic voting machines. Members insert voting cards into one of the devices located throughout the House chamber.

En Bloc Package: Several amendments offered together, by unanimous consent, affecting more than one part of a measure.

Enacting Clause: Opening phrase of a bill giving it legal force: "Be it enacted by the Senate and House of Representatives of the United States of America in Congress assembled...."

Engrossed Measure: Official copy of a measure as passed by one chamber, including floor amendments, certified by the clerk of the House or the secretary of the Senate.

Enrolled Measure: Final official copy of a measure as passed in identical form by both chambers and printed on parchment. Measure is certified by the house of origin and signed by the Speaker of the House and the President *pro tempore* of the Senate before it is sent to the president.

Entitlement Program: Federal program guaranteeing specific benefits to individuals, businesses, or units of government that meet eligibility requirements.

Executive Session: Senate session devoted to the consideration of treaties or nominations. Also a term used to describe a chamber or committee session closed to the public.

Expenditures: General term for spending; often a synonym for outlays.

Fast-Track Procedures: Procedures that circumvent or speed up all or part of the legislative process. Some rule-making statutes prescribe expedited procedures for certain measures, such as trade agreements.

Filibuster: Tactic in the Senate to delay or defeat a measure by unlimited debate and other means.

First-Degree Amendment: Amendment offered directly to the text of a measure, or a substitute for such an amendment.

First Reading: Required reading of a bill or joint resolution to a chamber by title after its introduction.

Fiscal Year: Federal budget year, from October 1 through September 30. Fiscal year 2025 began October 1, 2024, and ends September 30, 2025.

Five-Minute Rule: House rule limiting debate on an amendment offered in the Committee of the Whole to five minutes for its sponsor and five minutes for an opponent. In practice, the Committee of the Whole permits the offering of pro forma amendments, each pro forma amendment allowing five more minutes of debate on an amendment.

Floor Manager: Member steering legislation through floor debate and the amendment process, usually a committee or subcommittee chair or ranking minority member.

General Debate: Initial debate in the Committee of the Whole on a measure, usually divided equally between majority and minority floor managers.

Germaneness: Rule in the House requiring that debate and amendments pertain to the same subject as the bill or amendment under consideration. In the Senate, germaneness is not generally required.

Hastert Rule: Archaic term for an informal practice of Republican Speakers to require support by "a majority of the majority" before bringing a bill to the House floor for a vote.

Hearing: A formal committee session in which witnesses present oral testimony (and written testimony, for the record) and members question them.

Hold: Senator's request to party leadership to delay or withhold floor action on a measure or executive business—understood as a senator's unwillingness to permit action on a measure by unanimous consent.

Hopper: Box on the Speaker's dais near the House clerk's desk where members place bills and resolutions for introduction.

Impoundment: Action or inaction by an executive official that delays or precludes the obligation or expenditure of budget authority. *See* Deferral; *see also* Rescission.

Insert: Amendment to add new language to a measure or another amendment.

Instruct Conferees: Formal, although not binding, action by one chamber urging its conferees to uphold a particular position in conference.

Intersession Recess: The period between adjournment *sine die* and the reconvening of Congress for the next session. *See* Intrasession Recess; *see aso* Recess.

Intrasession Recess: A period of adjournment within a session of Congress. *See* Intrasession Recess; *see also* Recess.

Joint Committee: A committee with membership from both chambers. Joint committees do not have legislative jurisdiction.

Joint Explanatory Statement: Statement appended to a conference report explaining the conference agreement and the intent of the conferees. Also called a Statement of Managers. *See also* Conference Report.

Joint Meeting: A ceremonial meeting of both houses of Congress, often to hear addresses from foreign dignitaries. Joint meetings are established by unanimous consent agreements in both houses. *See also* Joint Session.

Joint Resolution: Similar to a bill, though limited in scope (for example, to change a minor item in existing law). Becomes law when passed in identical form by both chambers and signed by the president. Also used to consider a constitutional amendment, which requires a two-thirds vote in each house but does not require the president's signature. Designated as *H.J. Res.* or *S.J. Res. See also* Bill.

Joint Session: A formal session of both houses of Congress for purposes of hearing an address from the president or to conduct formal business. A joint session requires that both houses adopt a concurrent resolution establishing the session. *See also* Joint Meeting.

Lame-Duck Session: Session of Congress held after the election but before the new Congress convenes.

Law: Act of Congress signed by the president or passed over a veto. *See* Public Law; *see also* Private Bill.

Legislative Day: Period from when a chamber meets after an adjournment until the time it next adjourns.

Line-Item Veto: A proposed presidential power to veto specific items in an appropriation bill without vetoing the whole measure.

Managers: Members responsible for leading legislation on a chamber floor or in discussion with the other chamber.

Mandatory Spending: *See* Direct Spending.

Mark: *See* Vehicle.

Markup: Meeting by a committee or subcommittee during which members offer, debate, and vote on amendments to a measure.

Minority, Supplemental, and Additional Views: Statements in a committee report presenting individuals' or groups' opinions on the measure.

Morning Business: In the Senate, routine business transacted at the beginning of the Morning Hour, or by unanimous consent throughout the day. *See* Morning Hour.

Morning Hour: In the Senate, the first two hours of a session following an adjournment, rather than a recess.

Motion to Instruct: Motion in either chamber directing its conferees to take a particular position in conference. Such instructions are not binding on the conferees.

Nomination: Appointment by the president to executive office or judicial office that is subject to Senate confirmation.

Obligation: Binding agreement by a government agency to pay for goods, products, or services.

Official Title: Statement of a measure's subject and purpose, which appears before the enacting clause. *See also* Popular Title.

Omnibus Bill: A measure that combines provisions on several unrelated subjects into a single measure. Examples include continuing appropriations resolutions that might contain two or more of the twelve annual appropriations bills.

Ordered Reported: Committee's formal action to report a measure to its chamber.

Original Bill: A measure drafted by a committee and introduced by its chair when reported to the chamber. It is not referred back to the committee after introduction.

Outlays: Payments to liquidate obligations.

Parliamentary Inquiry: Member's question posed on the floor to the presiding officer, or in committee or subcommittee to the chair, about a pending procedural situation.

Passed: Term for approval of bills and joint resolutions.

PAYGO (Pay-As-You-Go): Process by which direct spending increases or revenue decreases must be offset so that the deficit is not increased or the surplus reduced.

Perfecting Amendment: Amendment that alters, but does not completely substitute or replace, language in another amendment. *See* Amendment Tree.

Pocket Veto: President's withholding of approval of a measure after Congress has adjourned, preventing Congress's ability to override a veto.

Point of Order: Objection to a current proceeding, measure, or amendment because the proposed action violates a rule of the chamber, written precedent, or rule-making statute.

Popular Title: The name by which a measure is known. Also known as the short title. *See also* Official Title.

Post-Cloture Debate: A provision of Senate Rule XXII providing for up to 30 hours consideration (all activity including debate, votes, and quorum calls) after cloture has been invoked. *See also* Cloture.

Postpone: There are two types of motions to postpone: to postpone (indefinitely) kills a proposal, but to postpone to a day certain merely changes the day or time of consideration.

Preamble: Introductory language in a bill preceding the enacting clause. It describes the reasons for and intent of a measure. In a joint resolution, the language appears before the resolving clause. In a concurrent or simple resolution, it appears before the text.

Precedence: Order in which amendments or motions may be offered and acted upon.

Precedent: Ruling by a presiding officer that becomes part of the chamber's procedural record.

President *pro tempore*: Presiding officer of the Senate in the absence of the vice president; usually the majority-party senator with the longest period of continuous service.

Previous Question: Nondebatable House (or House committee) motion, which, when agreed to, cuts off further debate, prevents the offering of additional amendments, and brings the pending matter to an immediate vote.

Private Bill: A measure that generally deals with an individual matter, such as a claim against the government, an individual's immigration, or a land title. Private bills are considered in the House via the Private Calendar on the first and third Tuesdays of each month.

Privilege: Attribute of a motion, measure, report, question, or proposition that gives it priority status for consideration.

Pro Forma Amendment: Motion whereby a House member secures five minutes to speak on an amendment under debate, without offering a substantive amendment. The member moves to "strike the last word" or "strike the requisite number of words." The motion requires no vote and is deemed automatically withdrawn at the expiration of the five minutes. *See also* Five-Minute Rule.

Pro Forma Session: Session of either the House or Senate with little or no business conducted. Pro forma sessions became particularly controversial in the Senate after 2007 when used to prevent the president from making recess appointments.

Proxy Vote: The practice of permitting a member to cast the vote of an absent colleague.

Public Debt: Amounts borrowed by the Treasury from the public or other government fund or account.

Public Law: Act of Congress signed by the president or passed over a veto. It is designated by the letters *P.L.* and numbers noting the Congress and the numerical sequence in which the measure was signed; for example, P.L. 112-7 was an act of Congress in the 112th Congress and was the seventh measure signed by the president (or passed over a veto) during that Congress.

Queen-of-the-Hill Rule: A special rule that permits votes on a series of amendments, usually complete substitutes for a measure, but directs that the amendment receiving the greatest number of votes prevails.

Quorum: Minimum number of members required to conduct business (default of 218 in the House; 100 in the Committee of the Whole; 51 in the Senate).

Quorum Call: A procedure for determining whether a quorum is present.

Ramseyer Rule: House rule requiring committee reports to show changes a reported measure would make in current law. *See also* Cordon Rule.

Ranking Member: The highest ranking minority member of a committee.

Recede: Action by one chamber to withdraw from its previous position during conference consideration or amendments between the chambers.

Recess: Temporary interruption or suspension of a committee or chamber meeting. In the House, the Speaker is authorized to declare recesses. In the Senate, the chamber may recess rather than adjourn at the end of the day so as not to trigger a new legislative day. The term is also used to refer to a period in which the House or Senate has adjourned pursuant to a concurrent resolution. *See* Intrasession Recess; *see also* Intersession Recess.

Recess Appointment: A temporary presidential appointment made during a recess of the Senate without the advice and consent of the Senate, provided for in Article II, Section 3 of the Constitution.

Recommit: To send a measure back to the committee that reported it. A motion to recommit without instructions kills a measure; a motion to recommit with instructions proposes to amend a measure. In the House, the motion may be offered just before vote on final passage. In the Senate, the motion may be offered at any time before a measure's passage.

Reconciliation: Process for changing existing laws to conform revenue and spending levels to the limits set in a budget resolution. Limited to 20 hours of debate in the Senate.

Reconciliation Instruction: A provision within a Budget Resolution directing committees to report legislation that changes existing law. Such instructions are a precondition to the consideration of a reconciliation bill.

Reconsider: Parliamentary practice allowing a chamber one opportunity to review its action on a motion, amendment, measure, or any other proposition.

Refer: Assignment of a measure to committee.

Report/Reported: Formal submission of a measure by a committee to its parent chamber.

Reprogram: Shifting funds within the same appropriation account from one program to another. *Contrast* with Transfer.

Rescission: Cancellation of budget authority previously provided by Congress.

Resolution/Simple Resolution: Sentiment of one chamber on an issue, or a measure to carry out the administrative or procedural business of the chamber. Does not become law. Designated as *H. Res.* or *S. Res.*

Resolving Clause: First section of a joint resolution that gives legal force to the measure when enacted: "Resolved by the Senate and House of Representatives of the United States of America in Congress assembled…."

Revenues: Federal income from individual and corporate income taxes, social insurance taxes, excise taxes, fees, tariffs, and other sources collected under the sovereign powers of the federal government.

Rider: Colloquialism for an amendment unrelated to the subject matter of the measure to which it was attached.

Rise: Motion in the Committee of the Whole during the amendment stage that has the effect of terminating or suspending debate on the pending matter.

Rise and Report: Conclusion of proceedings in the Committee of the Whole. The Committee of the Whole sends the measure it has been considering back to the House for final disposition.

Roll-Call (Record) Vote: A vote in which members' positions are recorded by name.

Rule, Closed: Permits general debate for a specified period of time but generally prohibits amendments.

Rule, Modified Closed: Permits general debate for a specified period of time, but limits amendments to those designated in the special rule or the House Rules Committee report accompanying the special rule. May preclude amendments to particular portions of a bill. Also called a structured rule.

Rule, Modified Open: Permits general debate for a specified period of time, and allows any member to offer amendments consistent with House rules subject only to an overall time limit on the amendment process and a requirement that amendments be pre-printed in the *Congressional Record*.

Rule, Open: Permits general debate for a specified period of time and allows any member to offer an amendment that complies with the standing rules of the House.

Rule, Self-Executing: If specified, the House's adoption of a special rule may also have the effect of amending or passing the underlying measure. Also called a "hereby" rule.

Rule, Structured: Another term for a modified closed rule. *See* Rule, Modified Closed.

Score: Congressional Budget Office's determination of the budgetary impact of legislation.

Second: The number of members required to indicate support for an action, such as calling for a vote.

Second-Degree Amendment: An amendment to an amendment. Also called a perfecting amendment. See *Amendment Tree.*

Second Reading: Required reading of a bill or joint resolution to a chamber: in the House, in full before floor consideration in the House or Committee of the Whole (usually dispensed with by unanimous consent or special rule); in the Senate, by title only, before referral to a committee. Under Senate Rule XIV, if objection is made to further proceedings on the measure after the second reading, it is placed directly on the calendar.

Seniority System: Preferential treatment based on length of service in the chamber or on a congressional committee.

Special Orders: Speeches in the House after legislative business has concluded for the day, for up to 60 minutes.

Rule, Special: A House resolution reported by the Rules Committee that sets the terms for debate, amendment, and votes on a measure.

Stage of Disagreement: Stage at which one chamber formally disagrees with an amendment proposed by the other chamber and insists on its own amendment. A measure generally cannot go to conference until this stage is reached.

Star Print: A reprint of a measure, amendment, or committee report to correct errors in a previous printing. The first page carries a small black star.

Statement of Managers: *See* Joint Explanatory Statement.

Strike: Amendment to delete a portion of a measure or an amendment.

Strike and Insert: Amendment that replaces text in a measure or an amendment.

Strike the Last Word/Strike the Requisite Number of Words: Means of obtaining time to speak on an amendment without actually offering a substantive change. Also called a pro forma amendment. *See* Pro Forma Amendment.

Substitute Amendment: Amendment that replaces the entire text of a pending amendment. *See* Amendment Tree.

Supplemental Appropriations Act: An appropriations act that provides additional budget authority during the current fiscal year when regular appropriations are insufficient.

Surplus: Excess of revenues over outlays.

Suspension of the Rules: Expeditious House procedure for passing noncontroversial measures. Requires a two-thirds vote of those present and voting, after forty minutes of debate, and does not allow floor amendments.

Table/Lay on the Table: Motion preventing further consideration of a measure, amendment, or motion, thus killing it.

Tax Expenditure: Loss of revenue attributable to an exemption, deduction, preference, or other exclusion under federal tax law.

Third Reading: Required reading of a bill or joint resolution to chamber before vote on final passage; usually a pro forma procedural step.

Transfer: Shifting funds from one appropriation account to another, as authorized by law. *Contrast* with Reprogram.

Trust Funds: Accounts designated by law as trust funds for receipts and expenditures earmarked for specific purposes.

Unanimous Consent: Refers to the absence of objection by any senator.

Unanimous Consent Agreement/Time Limitation Agreement: Senate device to expedite legislation by spelling out the process for considering a proposal.

Vehicle/Legislative Vehicle: A legislative measure that is being considered.

Veto: Disapproval by the president of a bill or joint resolution (other than a joint resolution proposing a constitutional amendment). *See* Veto Override; *see also* Pocket Veto.

Veto Override: Passage of legislation vetoed by the president may occur by two-thirds recorded voted of each chamber. *See* Veto; *see also* Pocket Veto.

Views and Estimates: Annual report from each House and Senate committee on budgetary matters within its jurisdiction, submitted to its chamber's Budget Committee before drafting a concurrent resolution on the budget.

Voice Vote: A method of voting where members who support a question call out "aye" in unison, after which those opposed answer "no" in unison. The chair decides which position prevails.

Well: Open space at the front of the House and Senate chambers between members' seats and the podium. Members in the House may speak from lecterns in the well.

Yeas and Nays: A vote in which members respond "aye" or "no" on a question. Their names are called in alphabetical order.

Index

References are to chapter and section number (e.g., 3.F refers to section F in chapter 3).

About Legis1

Legis1 is a next-generation legislative intelligence platform that leverages advanced AI and robust analytics to deliver unparalleled insight into the inner workings of Congress and the government affairs industry. Designed for professionals seeking to build connections, harness data-driven insights, and maximize impact, Legis1 transforms complex political data into actionable knowledge.

Legis1's intuitive interface is built around three core capabilities:

Data-Driven Insights:

- Leverage integrated data, advanced analytics, and AI tools to identify patterns, predict congressional activity, and assess the policy landscape around customizable issue areas
- Analyze member and committee communications and messaging trends using AI-enhanced analytics and keyword searches of more than 1 million communications from 1998-present
- Analyze member offices and committees by legislative effectiveness, voting record, staff compensation, turnover, and experience

Connection Building:

- Map influence through an expansive, interlinked network of Member of Congress, congressional staffers, witnesses, government affairs professionals, donors, and lobbyists
- Study the connections and capital flows between lobbyists, their clients, and Congress
- Access directories of staffers and lobbyists with profiles featuring issue areas and contact information (email, phone, address)

Research Efficiency:

- Access 20+ years of legislative history and congressional hearings, complete with AI-generated summaries and searchable transcripts
- Track every local and national news article mentioning Members of Congress, analyze media coverage by lawmaker and media outlet, and assess social media following and reach
- Explore 20+ years of congressional witness testimony and Member questions, complete with analytics and sentiment analysis

With Legis1, go beyond rhetoric and uncover the reality of political decision-making — driven by data, enhanced with AI, and grounded in facts.

Request a Demo

About The Sunwater Institute

The Sunwater Institute is a nonpartisan, nonprofit think tank dedicated to strengthening the foundations of liberal democracy through interdisciplinary science, technology, and open dialogue.

Guided by the belief that transparency, civic participation, and informed debate are essential to a thriving democracy, Sunwater brings together thought leaders and publishes research and practical resources that elevate public policy conversations. From demystifying the legislative process to equipping citizens with the tools to engage effectively, Sunwater helps individuals and institutions alike navigate and shape American governance today.

Explore More Sunwater Books

Sunwater publishes a growing collection of authoritative guides on lawmaking, advocacy, and civic engagement, including:

- *Testifying Before Congress* — A practical guide to assist witnesses and their organizations in preparing and delivering Congressional testimony

- *Citizen's Handbook for Influencing Elected Officials* — A rare insider's view of how legislators make decisions and what kinds of advocacy actually influence them

- *Congressional Deskbook* — A comprehensive guide to Congress

- *The Legislative Drafter's Desk Reference* — Best practices for drafting clear, effective legislative language

- *Media Relations Handbook* — Guidance for public officials, advocates, and experts on communicating a message and working with the press

Learn more about Sunwater's full catalog of publications by scanning the QR code below.

Stay Informed

Scan the QR code below to sign up for Sunwater's newsletter and receive timely updates on new releases, expert commentary, and upcoming events.

www.ingramcontent.com/pod-product-compliance
Lightning Source LLC
Chambersburg PA
CBHW040255290326
41929CB00052B/3427